D1029377

# HERO OF TRAFALGAR

*The Story of*
LORD NELSON

# HERO OF TRAFALGAR

## The Story of
# LORD NELSON

*A. B. C. Whipple*

*Illustrated by William Hofmann*

RANDOM HOUSE · NEW YORK

THIS ONE IS FOR

# Christopher

All rights reserved under International and Pan-American Copyright
Conventions. Published in New York by Random House, Inc., and
simultaneously in Toronto, Canada, by Random House of Canada, Limited.
Manufactured in the United States of America

Designed by Guy Fleming

Library of Congress catalog card number: 63–7806

4 364

# CONTENTS

# HERO OF TRAFALGAR

*The Story of*
LORD NELSON

# I

## A DASH THROUGH
## THE NIGHT

HE PORTSMOUTH ROAD RAN FROM London down through lowlands to the sea. Across country it rose and dipped with the rolling hills; through villages and towns it twisted past market places and cobbled squares. Even at night the people along the Portsmouth Road were accustomed to hearing the thud of horses' hoofs and the rattle of wooden wheels as the London stagecoach rolled by. But on the night of September 13, 1805, more than a century and a half ago, Englishmen waked and stirred in their beds as a strange carriage raced past their houses and off into the darkness, down the road to Portsmouth.

Many Englishmen were wakeful that night anyway. Perhaps it was because of the date—Friday the 13th. Perhaps it was because no one along the Portsmouth Road was very far from the beaches where the invasion troops might land when the enemy came. Everyone knew that thousands of picked troops were massed on the French shores, just across the English Channel. France, under Emperor Napoleon Bonaparte, was at war with England, and the invasion troops waited only for his command to cross the Channel and swarm ashore on the beaches of England. So the night seemed darker than usual, the wind seemed to howl louder than usual, and the hurrying, clattering carriage seemed to sound the alarm all along the Portsmouth Road. England was on the eve of one of the greatest battles in history.

If any one of those who woke and wondered at the urgent sound had been able to look inside the passing carriage, he would have seen a lone, frail figure of a man bracing himself with his left arm as the carriage lurched from side to side. The man wore the uniform of a vice admiral in the Royal Navy. His empty right sleeve was pinned to his coat. His right eye was blind. And on his face, as he peered out at the black trees and dark windows flashing past, was all the loneliness—and the determination—of a man who had left everything he loved in order to go into battle and risk his life for his country.

Anyone in England who saw that face and that slight, straight figure knew immediately who it was. If, as everyone expected, Napoleon gave the signal and the French mounted their invasion of

England, this was the one man who might be able to stop them. Anyone who saw him realized that the fate of England rode with this half-blind, one-armed man, racing through the chill September night down to Portsmouth and the sea.

He was Viscount Horatio Nelson, the greatest naval hero his country ever produced. This is his story.

# II

# THE TWELVE-YEAR-OLD
# SAILOR

NE OF THE FIRST SOUNDS HORATIO
Nelson heard as a baby was a
soft murmur that came through
his bedroom window in the quiet,
hazy September days of 1758. It
was the sound of the sea. The sea
washed against the sandy shores of Norfolk, near
his home. It sent swirling fogs in across the land,
and always there was the tang of salt in the air.
Soon the sighing of the summer surf changed to
the roar and boom of the winter gales, as the
North Sea swept, straight from the North Pole,
down on the Norfolk coast. Ice floes piled up
along the beach, and huge tides swelled over the
marshes, and the wind banged at the dormer
windows of young Horatio Nelson's house.

The house was called the Parsonage, which
meant that it was the home of the minister of the
little church at Burnham Thorpe, one of the
villages in Norfolk County. Horatio's father, the

Reverend Edmund Nelson, was the minister. He and his wife had eleven children, but three of them died as babies. Horatio was the sixth child, and he could remember only the four brothers and three sisters who grew up with him. The Parsonage was a rambling old house in the shape of an L, made up of two or three cottages that had been added to each other long ago. Tile roofs slanted steeply in many directions. And when winter finally gave way to the warmth of spring, the fruit trees along one wall burst into thousands of flowers.

With springtime the Nelson children poured out across the countryside. Sheep grazed just beyond the white fence around the Parsonage. The green hills rolled away toward the seashore, and not far from the house there was a high sand dune where a signal mast stood. Young Horatio spent many hours there, looking out across the North Sea at the sparkling white sails of the ships forever passing up and down the coast. Some turned and came in around the point to the nearby seaport town of King's Lynn. Barges moved slowly inland along the canals. Windmills creaked and turned with the shifting breezes. Long-legged herons stalked through the marshes. Fishermen carried their nets and baskets down to the sea. And along the sandy shores were the thousands of shells and stones and fish scales and pieces of driftwood that always make the water's edge an adventure for any young boy.

But Horatio Nelson's life was not all explorations along the beaches and daydreaming on the high sunny dunes. His father was strict and stern. No one in the Parsonage lay in bed long after dawn, and at night everyone, young or old, was in bed by nine. Mr. Nelson saw to it that each child learned to sit so straight that his back did not touch the back of the chair. Weak eyes, he said, were no excuse for glasses. The salary of a minister was barely enough to supply food for the family of eight children, and there was never enough heat in the drafty old Parsonage when the wild winter winds swept down off the North Sea. Then, when Horatio was nine years old, his mother died.

It was Christmas time in 1767. Even when he was a grown man many years later, Horatio Nelson said that he could not think back to that winter without tears coming to his eyes. His eldest sister, twelve-year-old Susannah, had to take over the job of being mother to the other children, including the baby Catherine. A cheerful old lady named Blackett helped out as the "nurse," and sometimes one of the older local girls came in to do some of the housework. But the baby and five-year-old brother Edmund took up most of their time, and Horatio and the other older Nelson children were left to take care of themselves.

Horatio walked through rain or snow to the next

town to school, where he boarded for the term. One morning when the snow was very deep, Horatio and his older brother William started out to return to school for the term, but came home to report to their father that the road was apparently impassable. The Reverend Mr. Nelson told them to try again, and not to give up unless they found they really could not get through. They tried again. The road was almost lost under the huge drifts. William, the older brother, decided they should turn back. But Horatio persuaded him to keep on. "Remember," he said, "it was left to our honor." They got through.

One of his school friends remembered Horatio as a quiet, frail boy in a green coat who urged his classmates to man the village pump and make rivers in the street so he could sail his paper boats. He was twelve years old when he happened to read in a local newspaper the story that decided his career.

The newspaper reported that the warship *Raisonable*, sixty-four guns, was fitting out to go to sea and take her part in the war with Spain. Her commander would be Captain Maurice Suckling. Captain Suckling was Horatio's uncle.

Horatio's father was ill and had gone to the town of Bath, which was famous for its health-giving waters. Horatio felt he was too young to write the kind of letter that would persuade his father to let him go to sea. Instead, he talked his thirteen-year-old brother into doing it for him. Their father thought it over for a long time. Horatio was young, but in those days many boys his age went to sea as cabin boys and in similar posts. And the Reverend Mr. Nelson could be sure that Uncle Maurice would keep an eye on the young sailor. There would be one less mouth to feed at the Parsonage, and Horatio might get started early on a career in the British navy. Mr. Nelson finally passed the request on to Captain Suckling.

Back came an answer that must have made the twelve-year-old boy wonder if he had made the wrong decision. Like many others in the family, Uncle Maurice called Horatio "Horace." Now he wrote: "What has poor Horace done, who is so weak, that he above all the rest should be sent to rough it out at sea? But let him come; and the first time we go into action, a cannon-ball may knock off his head, and provide for him at once." Horatio's father explained that his uncle was joking, and would be glad to have him aboard the *Raisonable*. So Horatio prepared to go to sea.

But the *Raisonable* was not ready for sea yet. Horatio went back to school for a few more weeks. Then, on a cold morning in March, the message came: the *Raisonable* was taking stores and crew aboard. It was time to go.

Horatio packed his few extra clothes in a small duffle bag. He said good-bye to his brothers and sisters, then climbed into the stagecoach with his father and rattled away toward London. Father and son stayed overnight in London, and then the Reverend Mr. Nelson saw young Horatio to the Chatham stagecoach, where the two said good-bye. Chatham was only a few miles down the Thames River from London, and Horatio's father expected the boy's uncle to meet him there.

But there was no one to meet him when the coach arrived in Chatham. The seaport town was all bustle and confusion, and everyone was too busy to take notice of a twelve-year-old boy wandering alone along the water front. Horatio could find no one who knew which of the many ships in the harbor was the *Raisonable*. When he finally did locate a man who pointed her out, there was no one who would agree to row him out to her.

A naval officer walking along the docks happened to notice the small figure standing on the wharf and looking out to sea. The boy's collar was turned up against the biting March wind. His knees shook and his lip quivered. Perhaps the officer remembered the day he first left his home and family and found himself alone in a strange harbor town. He took the shivering boy to his house for some food and warmth, and saw to it that Horatio was rowed out to his ship.

Then Horatio found that Captain Suckling was not expected aboard for a few more days. No one knew of the berth promised for his nephew. The few members of the crew aboard were busy loading stores and readying ship. For the rest of the day, while the sailors ignored him, the lonely boy walked about the decks of the *Raisonable*. He studied her rigging and the other ships around her in the harbor, and wondered what the future held in store for him.

# III

---

## "I WILL BE A HERO"

ORATIO NELSON'S UNCLE WAS A gruff old sea dog. When he finally came aboard the *Raisonable* he had little time to devote to his nephew. The ship was made ready. All hands were assigned to their watches. Sails were broken out. The men marched around the capstan and chanted as the anchor chain came clanking up through the hawsehole. The *Raisonable* began to move slowly. She picked up speed, as her sails filled with wind, and moved out past Sheerness and into the English Channel. Young Horatio Nelson was already too busy to spend any time looking back on the England he was leaving, at twelve years of age, to start his career.

The English Channel can be one of the roughest bodies of water in the world. The *Raisonable* was not long out of the harbor before she started rolling, pitching and shuddering as she plunged into the head-on seas. As a midshipman, Horatio was crowded into a tiny cabin area with so many others that there was barely room to swing a hammock. On the first windy night many of the other new boys were seasick. So was Nelson. The ship was battened down, with every opening closed to keep out the flying spray. As everyone grew sicker, the air itself became nauseating.

Through the ship's thick sides could be heard the pounding of the sea, the crash of the waves and the howling of the wind. Inside the cabin there was the moaning and the retching of seasick sailors. Young Horatio Nelson learned what it took to be a sailor on that first stormy night at sea.

In the next few days and weeks he learned a great deal more. He learned his way about the floating world of his warship. He learned how hard it was to climb out on a wet yardarm high over the roaring sea on a stormy night. He learned how the British navy recruited and treated its men. He learned how the men sometimes rebelled, and what happened to them when they did. Above all, he learned to be a naval officer in the finest tradition of the best navy in the world.

The ship on which young Horatio sailed had been captured from the French twelve years earlier. That was why she carried the French name of *Raisonable*. To a boy going to sea for the first time she was a huge ship, with masts so high they made him dizzy and sails that seemed to cover the sky. She carried row on row of big guns along her sides—sixty-four of them, almost enough for a boy to lose count. Yet the big ship always seemed crowded below. In the quarters Horatio Nelson shared with other young midshipmen there was space only for his hammock and scarcely any room for stowing his gear. But he was far better off than the seamen in the lower decks. Down below the waterline, there were no portholes and the only light came from lanterns even in the middle of the day. The men quartered there were so crowded that they could lie in their hammocks and not even swing to the roll of the ship, so closely were they packed.

In fact, a warship in those days did not have enough room for the entire crew to sling hammocks at any one time. The crew was divided into watches, with half the men working while the other half rested or slept. And it was while on watch that Horatio Nelson learned to be a sailor in the British Royal Navy.

Much of his work was done aloft, on yardarms higher than a housetop. From the deck he was forced to climb up the rigging until the sailors below looked like midgets. There he could stand on a tiny platform until he got used to the fact that he was swinging far out over the water with every roll of the ship. Then he had to crawl out

along the yardarm, hanging on as he tried to keep from missing the footrope and falling while the ship plunged under him. At first, like all new hands, he tried to work with one arm, using the other to hang on for dear life, as he furled sail. But soon an officer was shouting at him, or swinging a knotted rope at him, to make him work with both hands.

Sometimes, when the breeze was light and the ship ran along on an even keel, it was pleasant to stand on the footrope and lean over the yardarm, looking down at the blue sea swishing by and daydreaming as the wind sang softly in the rigging. But then there were nights when all was black and the gale screamed and the sails thundered and the ship plunged so that the masts seemed to keep going right on over into the water. On nights like this Horatio Nelson had to work harder and faster than ever. If he did not, the ship might sink in the storm, taking all hands down with her.

Often the footropes and yards were covered with ice. If a sailor's fingers, numb with cold, fumbled and let go, he could pitch from the swaying footrope into the empty blackness below. If the ship were at that moment swinging out over the sea, he would drop like a cannonball and sink so deep that he could not hold his breath long enough to struggle back to the surface. Even if he did, there was little chance that the ship could come about and find him in the dark, stormy waters. His cries would not be heard above the shrieking of the storm.

But the sailor who fell into the sea and drowned died a less painful death than the one who plunged onto the deck. A fall like this was enough to break nearly every bone in a man's body, and the ship's surgeon could do little but try to comfort him through his hours of agony until he died. It was a very lucky sailor who happened to fall into a sail. If his comrades worked fast, they could haul him back onto the footrope, still alive but scared within an inch of his life.

Sometimes it was just as dangerous on deck. In a pitching sea one of the huge guns could break loose from the ropes that held it to the gun port at the ship's side. Each gun weighed hundreds of pounds and was set on wheels so it could be rolled back and forth at its port. When one broke loose and slewed around, the iron monster could roll the length or width of the deck, crushing anything in its way. The only way to stop it was to get a long iron bar under the gun and heave it over on its side. Only a brave man would try that on a slippery, rolling deck.

When the weather grew rough and cold, there was always the chance of being struck by a shipmate falling from above. And when the seas rose higher and the ship plunged her bow under the towering waves, the hissing green water poured aboard and swept the length of the deck. Any sailor who was not ready to grab hold of something could be picked up like a cork in this boarding sea and carried over the rail.

There were plenty of men aboard Horatio Nelson's ship who had not joined up willingly. If the navy had waited for volunteers, it would never have been able to complete a crew for any of its warships. In those days a man could be walking the streets of a port town like Chatham or Liverpool one minute and, the next thing he knew, wake up in a hammock aboard a ship—after being knocked unconscious and kidnaped by a "press gang." These press gangs were roving bands authorized to capture men for service as sailors.

A man was not safe even if he were serving aboard a merchant ship. The ship could be boarded by a navy press gang, and the sailors from the merchant vessel could be hustled aboard a warship putting out to sea. There was no law against this in England, except the one that stated that press gangs could board only the ships returning home and had to leave enough sailors aboard to work the merchant ship into port.

About half of a warship's crew was made up of men who had been caught like this and forced into the navy. Others had been "drafted" by the officials of their towns, who had been ordered to provide men for the navy. Often the local officials sent beggars, thieves, pickpockets and juvenile delinquents whom they were happy to be rid of. When these men came aboard, one sailor wrote: "Stand clear! Every finger was fairly a fishhook; neither chest nor bed nor blanket nor bag escaped their sleight-of-hand thievery."

It was a rough and rebellious crew that manned most ships of the British navy in those days. And the officers used rough methods to keep them working. The seaman's "on watch" usually started with the shriek of the boatswain's whistle and the bellow of the mate: "All hands ahoy!" and "Up all hammocks ahoy!" Every man moved fast; if he did not, the mate "started" him with the flick of a knotted rope's end. When the work was not dangerous, it was long and dreary: scrubbing decks, tarring ropes, painting the ship's sides, shifting sail to make the most of every slant of wind.

For their labor the men were paid what amounted to a few dollars a month. And they did not receive that until they were released, sometimes after years of service. The food was often spoiled and there was usually not enough of it. Many of the officers believed that the only thing that could make good seamen was the harshest form of discipline. Any sailor who moved too slowly or grumbled over the work or the food was "corrected" by the whistling end of the knotted rope or the heavy end of a marlinespike.

There were even navy regulations against swearing. An ordinary seaman caught using profanity was forced to wear a heavy wooden collar and pace up and down the deck until he was ready to drop. One captain added two 32-pound shots to the collar and nearly broke the man's neck.

If a sailor made the mistake of talking back to a superior or falling asleep on watch, he received far sterner punishment. Taken below and chained, he was given a length of rope and ordered to make his own cat-o'-nine-tails. Then he was taken on deck, because in the crowded quarters below decks there was "not enough room to swing a cat." On deck the sailor was stripped to the waist. His wrists were tied and hoisted. Then he was lashed with the cat he had made, until his back was a bloody pulp. The bleeding back was doused with salt water, partly to add to the punishment but mostly to clean the wounds. Aboard British naval ships in the days when Horatio Nelson went to sea, this was an almost everyday occurrence.

Often the men rebelled, in hidden ways and in the dark of the night. An officer would fall down a companionway because someone had left a bucket on the steps. A marlinespike would drop from aloft and knock an unpopular mate unconscious. A 32-pound cannonball would roll the length of the deck, thundering down on an officer and crushing him against the rail if he did not jump quickly out of its path. Rarely were the seamen who tried such tricks of revenge found out. Woe to them when they were.

Some sailors who could not take the abuse and punishment tried to desert. It was not easy. Whenever a naval ship was in port or near land, a marine sentry was constantly on duty, patrolling the special "marine walk" to watch for any attempted desertion. If a man did get away, he was hunted down by the navy. If he was caught, his punishment was far worse than he had had before. A "run man" was taken back to his ship and sometimes "flogged through the fleet." As an example to others who might be planning to jump ship, he was taken in a boat and flogged before every vessel in the fleet. His punishment was usually halted before he died, and he was put back to work as soon as he could walk again.

With conditions like these—press gangs kidnaping the worst water-front riffraff and naval officers trying to beat them into submission—it was no wonder that there was sometimes open mutiny. In fact, the year 1797 was known in England as "the year of mutinies." That was the year when an entire British fleet mutinied at the great naval base at Spithead. The sailors refused to work the ships. Seizing the vessels, they sent the officers ashore. Not until the Admiralty agreed to raise their pay, improve their living conditions and even obtain the king's pardon for every mutineer, did the seamen allow the officers to return and assume command of the fleet.

This was the British navy that Horatio Nelson joined at the age of twelve. It was a navy in which few sailors wanted to serve, a navy for which crews had to be provided by press gangs. It was a navy that still underpaid and mistreated its men. And yet it was the greatest navy in the world. It was the navy that beat France, the navy that captured or sank all but one ship in the American navy in the Revolutionary War. It was the navy that made England a great power. It was the navy that kept Napoleon from conquering most of the world.

How could England's sailors be so poorly treated, so rebellious and such good sailors and fighters all at the same time? One good reason was Englishmen like Horatio Nelson. Like Nelson, the English sailors were great patriots. Every man was more than ready to die for his country. None could think of greater glory than bravery in battle for England. Even during the famous mutiny at Spithead, which happened while England was at war with France, the mutinous sailors announced that if the French fleet should put to sea, the mutiny would be postponed.

A more important reason was that the British navy was the first in the world to train its officers professionally instead of simply letting a wealthy or titled man, with no experience or training, purchase his officer's commission. British naval officers, schooled by harsh discipline, were proud of their competence. And this competence was recognized by their subordinates.

Most of the officers saw to it that discipline was maintained but with fairness to all, and these officers won the affection as well as the respect of their men. The commander in chief of the British navy at the time of the mutiny at Spithead was Lord Richard Howe. He was a tough old admiral, but he had always seen to it that everyone was treated fairly aboard his own ship. The sailors called him "Black Dick." This was, sailor fashion, their term of endearment. And when the Commander in Chief helped negotiate a settlement of their mutiny against the Admiralty, the sailors paraded Black Dick on their shoulders about the streets of Portsmouth as they celebrated their victory against the officers.

These were the years when a man's station in life was important, to the lower classes as well as the upper classes. The British seaman was brought up to respect what he called "his betters." In the British navy of that day a minister's son was a "gentleman" and therefore born to be an officer. He may have been poor, as Nelson was, but he expected to be an officer and a gentleman whether rich or poor. If another Norfolk boy who was a shoemaker's son joined the navy at the same time as Horatio Nelson, he expected to be a seaman, and never an officer. This was a simple fact of life accepted by all. The seaman's station aboard a warship was forward, while "his betters," the officers, were stationed aft.

So twelve-year-old Horatio Nelson was rated a midshipman, an officer candidate. With the other young gentlemen he was stationed in the gun room instead of the midshipmen's cockpit. The cockpit was on the orlop, or lowest, deck—below the ship's waterline. It was the home of the older midshipmen, who were not gentlemen and would probably not rise any higher in rank. The cockpit was famous for the rowdy and raucous life the older midshipmen lived. It was not considered a proper place for a boy not yet in his teens who was on his way to becoming an officer. Instead, the gentlemen midshipmen were quartered with the gunner on the gun deck, where portholes let in some light and where the air—and the company— were cleaner. The gunner, who commanded the men manning the ship's guns, had no more chance than the older midshipmen of rising higher in rank. But he was already of higher rank than they. And most gunners were good, steady men who could be counted on to be firm and fair and good teachers to the young gentlemen learning their way about the ship.

## "I Will Be a Hero"

Horatio Nelson learned his ship well for five months. But he did not see action aboard the *Raisonable*. The war fever quieted down and the ship was paid off. Horatio's uncle was transferred to the *Triumph*, a guardship in the River Thames. Captain Suckling did not forget his nephew. He spoke to a former shipmate, Captain John Rathbone, who was now master of a trading vessel bound out for the West Indies. Could a berth be found for a young man who wanted to learn more than he could aboard a guardship in the Thames?

Soon Horatio Nelson sailed out across the Atlantic aboard the merchant vessel. So far he had known only the hills and marshes of Norfolk and the gray seas off England and Europe. Now his ship rolled gently through the brilliant blue waters of the Caribbean. He watched dazzling white islands rise out of the sea. He walked along pink beaches and listened to the wind sigh through palm trees and the water suck in and out of coral caves. He turned brown under the hot dry sun of the West Indies. At night he watched his ship's masts draw slow circles against a black tropical sky sparkling with millions of stars. He tasted West Indian rum, smelled tobacco drying, and listened to the chatter of parakeets and the crooning song of the natives in the soft evening air.

He came home to England a sun-bronzed, muscular young man who had learned one thing more that would help him greatly in his career. He later wrote: "I returned . . . with a horror of the Royal Navy, and with a saying then constant with the seamen, 'Aft the most honor, forward the better man.' " Many a sailor who served under Horatio Nelson in later years would be thankful that their commander gave as much consideration to the men forward as to the officers aft.

The first two steps in Nelson's education had been guided by his uncle. Now Nelson arranged a lesson on his own, and a grueling one it was. When he learned that the Royal Navy was sending an expedition to the Arctic, he volunteered. In fact he begged to serve aboard one of the two ships. He was accepted, and in June of 1773 the expedition set sail in search of a passage to the south seas. For nearly four months the expedition members lived in below-zero weather as their ships tried to find a passage through the fields of ice. They were lost in blizzards. Ice coated every inch of the rigging. They were caught in an ice jam and barely escaped being trapped for an extra year when at last the ice fields broke up.

One foggy morning Horatio Nelson and a companion decided to hunt some polar bear. They came upon one and Nelson's gun misfired. Still he advanced on the huge brute, trying to club it with the butt of his rifle. Only the booming of the ship's gun, signaling for them to return, saved Nelson from being killed by the bear. When

asked by the captain to explain his foolhardiness, he replied with an outthrust lip: "Sir, I wished to kill the bear that I might carry its skin to my father." The bear got away, and Nelson got a scolding. But the incident showed another side of Nelson's character: he was completely without fear.

Nelson had scarcely returned home and got the warmth back in his bones when he was off across the ocean again. This time he sailed down around Africa and the Cape of Good Hope. He was serving with a squadron on a voyage to Asia. His ship was the *Seahorse* and Nelson was still a midshipman. Aboard the *Seahorse* he learned more about stern British navy discipline. On this one voyage, the ship's records indicate, 200 men were lashed at the gratings and flogged. But it was an exotic voyage, to places of which few boys Horatio Nelson's age would do more than dream. The *Seahorse* raced across the "Roaring Forties," the blustery southern latitudes of the Indian Ocean, to the lonely St. Paul and Amsterdam Islands. Then they headed north for India. They called at Madras, sailed on up the Bay of Bengal to Calcutta. In the swollen, chocolate-brown Hooghly River Nelson could see bodies burning on the Hindu ghats at the river front. The sweltering stillness of India's heat settled over the ship. Everything was baked and breathless until the

*Seahorse* moved out into the Bay of Bengal again, bound west for Bombay, for Surat and for Basra. Then they turned back east with a convoy for Bombay and Madras. Next the squadron called at Trincomalee, on the beautiful island of Ceylon. Here, Nelson said, was "the finest harbor in the world." But it was also one of the most deadly, diseased places in the world.

Even during wartime in the eighteenth century, more sailors were killed by disease than by the enemy. Aboard a crowded, badly ventilated warship the men suffered from rheumatism, pneumonia and tuberculosis. The worst killer aboard ship was scurvy, a disease caused by lack of fresh fruits and vegetables. British doctors had found that it could be cured by lime juice (which led to the slang name "limey" for Englishman). But lime juice still was not standard fare on British naval vessels in the Indian Ocean.

The most dreaded shipboard killers in these years, especially in the tropics, were the fevers—typhoid fever, yellow fever and malaria. There were no known cures, and about the only treatment was quinine, which lowered the stricken man's temperature but did nothing to fight the disease itself. Now, en route from the beautiful harbor of Trincomalee to Bombay, Nelson came down with a raging fever. The symptoms indicate that it was malaria.

Quinine did little to help. The fever, added to

India's sweltering heat, quickly took the weight and muscle off the figure that had been so robust in the West Indies and the Arctic. Then came paralysis. The squadron's chief surgeon could do nothing; all he could recommend was that the patient be put aboard the first ship returning to England. That was the *Dolphin*, a new frigate with comfortable quarters that must have been welcome to the desperately sick young man. He was carried aboard, "almost a skeleton," as he remembered it later, and the *Dolphin* made ready to sail for England and home.

The voyage took six months. The cool air seemed to have no effect on the fever. Nelson wasted away even more, and few of those who were caring for him thought he could last much longer. But with agonizing slowness he began to grow a little better. The *Dolphin*'s captain, James Pigot, took pity on the suffering midshipman and spent hours trying to cheer him up. Finally, as the *Dolphin* rounded the Cape of Good Hope and made her slow way into northern waters, the young midshipman started to recover.

Nelson's near-death in India had an effect that lasted throughout his life. Never again was he the sturdy, strong, muscular young man who had returned from the West Indies and the Arctic. Always he would look short, slight and frail. Whenever he touched at tropical ports again, there was a recurrence of the old fever. But the experience had an even more profound effect on him mentally than physically. During the weary six-month voyage home he had more time for thinking than ever before. At first, when he was unable to throw off the gloom left by the fever, he "almost wished myself overboard."

Nelson's mental recovery finally came about in an odd way. One hot afternoon, as the *Dolphin's* sails slatted back and forth on an almost airless sea, the sallow-cheeked young man lay on his bunk and tried to think of his future. He might never be completely healthy again. He had been struck down in the prime of his youth, before he had even started the long climb of promotion in the Royal Navy. He could see nothing ahead but the bleak prospect of a sickly, useless life. But then, for no reason at all, as he described it later, the world and his outlook on it were transformed.

"A sudden glow of patriotism was kindled within me, and presented my King and Country as my patron," he later wrote. As this emotion surged through him, the young midshipman made a vow that would shape the course of his life—and of England's history. " 'Well then,' I exclaimed. 'I will be a hero. . . . I will brave every danger.' "

# I V

## TRIAL BY SEA

**B**Y THE TIME HE HAD RETURNED home, Nelson was up and about again. He refused to take any time off to regain his strength. Instead he applied for active duty immediately. He was appointed fourth lieutenant of the 64-gun ship *Worcester*, on convoy duty to the American colonies, which were fighting for their independence from England. So well did he perform his duties that within a few months he was made second lieutenant of another ship, the frigate *Lowestoffe*, assigned to the Jamaica station in the West Indies. He was eighteen years old, extremely young for an officer third in command of a frigate. But in one of the *Lowestoffe's* actions he showed why he was advancing so fast —and how well he was keeping the promise he had made to himself.

The *Lowestoffe* sailed out of Jamaica searching for American privateers. During the American

Revolution the British had little trouble with the navy of the American colonies, partly because the best officers and seamen of America were serving aboard the non-navy privateers which attacked and looted British merchant vessels. Many of the privateers concentrated on the West Indies, where British vessels were coming and going with supplies for the British troops stationed in the islands. The *Lowestoffe* patrolled the West Indies looking for privateers. And one stormy day the frigate overtook and captured a privateer schooner.

The seas were running high and the winds were making both ships roll heavily. The *Lowestoffe's* captain, William Locker, ordered the first lieutenant to take a boat across to the privateer and assume command. Shortly the lieutenant was back, with the excuse that the ocean was too rough to approach and board the privateer. Captain Locker looked about at the other officers and asked if any of them would like to make a try at it. Assuming that none would if his first lieutenant would not, the captain prepared to climb down into the tossing boat himself. At the gangway he found his second lieutenant, Horatio Nelson. "It is my turn, now," said the young lieutenant, "and if I return, then it will be yours." Nelson made it across to the schooner, accomplished the perilous boarding of the prize and was rewarded with the command of the privateer.

Similar actions of Nelson made him popular with

other captains. During this time his uncle, Captain Suckling, became comptroller of the Royal Navy and head of the Navy Board. Of course Horatio Nelson's prospects were helped by the fact that he was the nephew of so powerful a navy officer. But Nelson won his own way by his heroic actions. When Sir Peter Parker came out to the Jamaica station to take over the command, he quickly noticed the hard-working, eager young lieutenant and took him on his flagship, the *Bristol*, as a junior officer. Within a few months Nelson was second in command. And a few months later he had his own ship, the brig *Badger*. It was not long before he had achieved even greater glory. At twenty, he was a captain in the Royal Navy.

The young captain promptly volunteered for what sounded like an impossible expedition. Spain had declared war against Britain. That meant that Spain's colonies in Central America threatened Britain's islands in the West Indies. So a plan was conceived to meet this threat. An expedition would be mounted against one of Spain's strongest bases in the area, Fort San Juan in Nicaragua. The fort was on the San Juan River, near strategic Lake Nicaragua, which the British called "the Gibraltar of Spanish America." If the expedition succeeded, it would cut across the narrow section of Central America from the Atlantic to the Pacific. The British would divide Spain's possessions north from south, crippling Spain's strength in America.

Nelson's mission was to convoy the troops to the coast and put them ashore. Then he was to return to Jamaica. But he quickly discovered that the men had never been up a river like this. They had no idea where the enemy was, nor even how far they had to go to reach their main target, Fort San Juan. The planning back in London had gone wrong, and this was the worst time of year for such an assault. The dry season was nearly at an end, so there was scarcely any water in the river. The rainy season was about to commence, with downpours, floods and spreading fevers. Nelson decided that he could not simply put the men ashore and sail away. He supervised the landing, then left his ship and went up the river with the troops.

The expedition was a five-month-long nightmare. The men waded through swamps, poled and paddled their way up the twisting, shallow river, climbed ravines around impassable rapids and carved their way through the hot, dripping jungle. In some parts, where the river was wide, they nearly went blind from the glare of the sun above and the shimmering white sands below. In other parts the river was so narrow that the trees met overhead and only a sickly green haze penetrated at midday.

In the rain and dampness nothing would dry out. Men began to sicken and die—from yellow fever, from drownings, from snakes. One man screamed as he was hit by a huge snake hanging down from a tree; he was dead before the stretcher could be rushed to him. So many men died each day that there was not enough time to bury them. For nearly half a year this battle against the elements went on. More than 1,800 men took part in it; no more than 380 came back. Of the 200 from Nelson's ship who went up the river with him, exactly 10 returned.

When some of the men wanted to turn back, it was Nelson who kept urging them forward. When they reached the first enemy outpost, the fortified island of San Bartholomew, it was Nelson who led the attack and captured the fort. The army commander of the expedition later reported to headquarters: "I want words to express the obligation I owe to that gentleman. He was the first on every service, whether by night or day." But Nelson was not present for the final victory, the capture of Fort San Juan itself. A messenger brought orders for him to report back to Jamaica to assume command of another ship. The others carried on in Nelson's spirit and the fort was taken.

But by the time Nelson arrived in Jamaica, he had begun to pay for his heroism. The fever he first contracted in India had come back during the San Juan expedition. Again he was paralyzed. He had to be sent home to England for a long recuperation. Here he learned that heroism has its small rewards too. At Bath, England, where he

was trying the same health-giving waters his father had tried before, the young captain was surprised by the small fee charged by one of his doctors. He never forgot the doctor's reason. "Pray, Captain Nelson, allow me to follow what I consider my professional duty. Your illness, sir, was brought on by serving your King and Country, and believe me, I love both too well to be able to receive any more."

It was three months before Nelson was able to walk about again. But as soon as he was on his feet, he was back at the Admiralty in London, asking for another ship.

He was given the frigate *Albemarle* and assigned to convoy duty in stormy northern waters far different from those around Jamaica and along the San Juan River. Convoy duty was dreary, and the *Albemarle* was a slow and cranky ship. But when she was decommissioned, Nelson was presented with an extraordinary petition from his crew. If he was taking command of another ship, said the petition, his crew would gladly give up shore leave in order to transfer with him and continue to serve under him. Unhappily Nelson had to tell his men that he too was being given shore duty for a while.

His shore duty did not last long. Soon he was sailing back to the West Indies, in command of the 28-gun frigate *Boreas*. There he met and fell in love with a young widow named Frances Nisbet, who lived on the island of Nevis. They were married on March 11, 1785. Soon they went to England, with the widow's young son Josiah, to set up housekeeping in the Parsonage with the Reverend Edmund Nelson, Horatio's father.

If she had ever wondered, the new Mrs. Nelson quickly found that with her husband the sea came first. After a short period ashore, Captain Nelson was off again, as master of the 64-gun *Agamemnon*. England and France were fighting each other once more, and the *Agamemnon* took part in the successful siege of Toulon. This was followed by two battles in which Captain Horatio Nelson learned that heroism could exact an even higher price than he had paid before.

# V

## THE PRICE OF GLORY

HE SEAPORT TOWN OF CALVI LIES on the northwest shore of the famous island of Corsica, in the Mediterranean Sea. In 1794 it was a rich prize in the conflict between England and France. Many Corsicans wanted England to take the island away from France, but England could not do so without first defeating the French forces concentrated at such ports as Calvi. The town sat high on a cliff and was nearly impossible to attack from the sea. So Nelson picked out a landing beach a few miles west of Calvi and set about landing men and guns there to move overland. A fearful storm struck as the operation started, but the landings were completed despite huge waves sweeping onto the landing beach. Then the guns from the *Agamemnon* were hauled over a mountain pass and placed in position for the attack on the town.

At this point the French finally came to life and

launched a counterattack. Against the few British guns from the *Agamemnon,* the French defenders had a strong force that was determined to hold fast.

At 7:00 A.M. on July 12, while Captain Nelson was in a forward position supervising the placement of the *Agamemnon*'s guns, the French bombardment started. A shell struck a stone wall in front of him and sent a shower of sand, rocks and metal into his face and chest. It took some time to stop the bleeding, but the ship's surgeon assured Nelson that he had suffered only surface lacerations—except for his right eye.

For a while the doctors and Nelson himself thought that the eye would recover. Later, after Calvi had surrendered, Captain Nelson retired to the privacy of his cabin and got out a mirror. Holding his hand over one eye and then the other, he verified what he had feared: his right eye was fading into blindness. It would be six months before he knew for certain, but already he could guess that he would lose his right eye.

To his wife and to friends he wrote that such wounds of war were to be expected and that he was fortunate not to be more seriously hurt. In fact, he said, he suspected that graver wounds would come later.

Nelson was now thirty-nine years old. He had been promoted to admiral, though he did not know it. The news had not reached him at sea.

Then, on St. Valentine's Day, February 14, 1797, the young admiral established himself as one of history's greatest naval tacticians. Nelson was in command of the 74-gun *Captain*, sailing twenty-five miles off Portugal's Cape St. Vincent, in a fleet of fifteen ships of the line under the command of Sir John Jervis. The British fleet was bearing down on a Spanish fleet which had been sighted racing for the protection of Cádiz. As the British closed in from the north, they discovered that the Spanish fleet, with twenty-seven ships of the line, was nearly twice the size of their own. But the Spanish commander in chief had let his fleet become divided into two sections, and Jervis seized the advantage. If he could take on the two sections of the fleet, one at a time, he would not have to attack twenty-seven ships all at one time with his own fifteen.

Luck was with the British, for a while. The Spaniards tried to reunite their fleet, but there was not enough wind to accomplish it in time. Down came the British ships straight between the two Spanish fleets. Off to the east, between the British line and the coast, was the smaller Spanish force, and to the west was the larger. Jervis chose the larger. This meant there were still eighteen ships against his fifteen, but it was less of a handicap than twenty-seven against fifteen.

Then Jervis did a stupid thing. As his line of battle ran on down alongside the larger section of the Spanish fleet, he ordered his ships to keep running south, then to swing back and attack the Spanish, by tacking in succession. This meant that the whole British line would run down to the same point, then turn and run back north, just like a train rounding a turn. The maneuver followed an old, traditional plan of battle, but one that could not have worked in this case. As the British ships ran south away from the Spaniards, and before they could turn and come back into action, the Spaniards simply headed north. Then they got ready to turn east again, swinging behind the end of the British line while it was still running south to make its turn.

It was Nelson who first realized Jervis' error and decided to correct it. His ship, the *Captain*, was third from the end of the British line, and he could see some of the Spanish ships already putting their helms over to run across the gap as soon as the British line had run far enough south. Nelson knew that Jervis' tactics were standard and traditional, right out of the book. He also knew that to make any change in this plan on his own would be a grave breach of discipline. He could be court-martialed and discharged from the navy for such disobedience. But as he watched the Spaniards sail north while the British continued to sail south, Nelson realized what Jervis should have done. And he decided to do something about it himself.

What Jervis should have done was to turn each

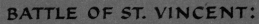

# BATTLE OF ST. VINCENT:
## February 14, 1797

A British ships of the
   line making their turn
B The larger Spanish force
C The smaller Spanish force
D Spanish ship separated
   from the smaller force
N Nelson's ship CAPTAIN swinging
   out of the line and heading north

ship around where it was, making his last ship his first ship. Then his fleet would have been in position to attack immediately, instead of sailing down and around a turning point. And what Nelson did was just that, but all by himself. Suddenly the *Captain* swung out of the line and ran north, plunging into battle alone against eighteen enemy ships.

It is to Jervis' credit that as soon as he saw what Nelson was doing he ordered the rest of the line to follow him and support him. The Spaniards, who had almost managed to reunite the two elements of their big fleet, were split again and could be attacked separately. This was possible only because Nelson had switched his commander's tactics in the middle of the engagement. The Spanish fleet was badly beaten, partly as a result of the lone attack of Nelson's ship, which had taken them completely by surprise.

Word of Nelson's daring and brilliance soon reached England. He was cheered by Englishmen everywhere as the hero of the Battle of St. Vincent, and rewarded by a title from a grateful king.

So it was Sir Horatio Nelson, Knight of the Bath, who a few months later led a small British fleet toward the Canary Islands. The British had learned that Spain was strengthening her naval base on Teneriffe, one of the Canary Islands lying off the coast of North Africa, and commanding the narrow entrance to the Mediterranean. If this were allowed to happen, every British ship in the Mediterranean would be trapped. So orders were dispatched to take Teneriffe.

As the fleet bore down on the islands, it ran into contrary winds. Then the winds died altogether, and strong currents swept the ships away from Teneriffe. It did not look like a favorable beginning for so difficult an operation.

On the evening of the landings, as the ships finally approached the island in the darkness, Admiral Nelson asked that the officer of the deck be summoned to his cabin. A young man entered and Nelson put an arm around him. The young man was his stepson, Lieutenant Josiah Nisbet, the only son of Nelson's wife. At Nelson's request Lieutenant Nisbet had been assigned to his ship. Now Josiah was dressed in battle uniform, ready to go ashore.

Nelson knew that a dangerous night lay ahead on the beaches of Teneriffe. In the council of war some of the officers had suggested that the island was lightly garrisoned and would offer little resistance. Nelson suspected that the assault would not be so easy. He doubted that they could any longer surprise the enemy, and he expected a fiery reception if the Spaniards were waiting for them. In fact, before calling in his stepson, he had made out his will.

Nelson himself had been ordered not to go ashore unless he found it necessary. But of course he found it necessary. So he could hardly order Josiah to stay aboard the ship. Instead he tried persuasion.

"Should we both fall, Josiah," he asked, "what would become of your poor mother?"

"Sir," Josiah replied, "I will go with you tonight if never again." Nelson argued no more.

It was 10:30 P.M. when the first troops started climbing down into the landing boats. The night was black, and the wind was driving sheets of rain almost horizontally. Beside the ships the small boats rose to the rail and dropped out of sight as the heavy swells of the sea rolled in toward the island. By 11:00 P.M. all the boats and one cutter, the *Fox*, had put off. Still there was no sound except that of the wind and the rain. So far, Teneriffe's defenders seemed unaware of the attackers rowing silently toward them through the night.

In a ship's boat in the central division of the attacking van rode Nelson. The boat surged under him as the oarsmen tried to stay on top of each swell sweeping toward the beach. As they drew nearer to the island, they could hear on either side the rumble and crash of breakers on the rocks. Only a short stretch of sandy beach near the center of the town of Santa Cruz was safe for landing, and even there the surf could be heard thundering onto the shore. Still there were no sounds save the wind, rain and surf. As the landing craft came nearly within gunshot of the town, a few dim lights could be made out. But there was no sign that the Spaniards knew of the invasion force creeping toward them.

Suddenly the sky was lit by the red trails of rockets soaring over the boats. Between the rockets came blue flares which threw an eerie pall over the scene. Around the boats the sea erupted in little fountains as the big guns on the shore tried to find the range. In the background, over the pounding of the surf, the roar of the wind and the thump of the guns, came a clanging chorus of church bells, signaling to the island that the battle was on. And over all the other sounds came the voice of Admiral Nelson yelling his command: *Go for the shore!*

Watching the rockets arch through the sky and cannonballs splash into the water around his boat, Nelson realized that the worst had happened. The enemy not only had expected the attack, but they had dug in their defenses and were sitting there prepared to wipe out the attackers. Before his boat hit the shore he knew that the assault had little chance of success. But he did not think of turning back. In the brief flashes of light from the rockets or flares, he could see that many of the boats were doomed even before they reached the island. Swept off course by the wind and the swells, they were plunging down onto the jagged rocks on either side of the town. Nothing could save them from foundering with all hands. Nelson's boat made it to the sandy shore. Everyone hit the beach and dashed for cover from the bullets and shells that were sweeping the water's edge.

Most of the shot covering the beach was grape— spraying volleys of musket balls that swept the area like buckshot. As Nelson stepped out of the boat and drew his sword, a shower of grapeshot struck him in the right elbow. The blow spun him around and knocked him to the ground. His first reaction was to grab with his good left hand for the sword that had fallen into the sand. It had belonged to his famous uncle, Captain Suckling, and Nelson considered it a good-luck token. But he was unable to get back on his feet, and the gush of blood from his wound rapidly weakened him until he scarcely knew what was happening.

The men in his boat had plunged on across the beach, searching for shelter from the defenders' fire. Nelson might have lain there and bled to death if it had not been for his stepson. Josiah Nisbet quickly noticed that Nelson was not with those who had crossed the beach, and he returned, looking for him. He found Nelson, lying in a pool of blood near the boat. Calling for help, Josiah collected five men and lifted his stepfather back into the boat. The surf had washed the boat far up onto the beach, and Josiah and his helpers had all they could do to shove it back into the water.

Josiah took a neckerchief and tied it tightly around Nelson's arm just above the wound, slowing the flow of blood. The boat started away from the beach, pitching high over the breakers and out toward the ship.

At that point the cutter *Fox*, which had left the ship at the same time as Nelson's boat, was struck and holed below the waterline. She started to sink, amid the screams of men floundering about in the storm-whipped water. As if at the sound of their cries, Nelson regained consciousness and sat up. Josiah was directing their course for the nearest ship. But Nelson looked across at the sinking *Fox* and ordered the rowers to go over and save the swimming sailors. Josiah argued with him, pointing out that if Nelson's bleeding were not tended by a doctor right away he might die. Nelson refused to listen. While he lay bleeding in the bottom of the boat, the oarsmen turned the boat and rowed over to the sinking cutter. It took almost half an hour to complete the rescue, but many of the *Fox*'s men were saved.

By the time the boat reached Nelson's ship, the *Theseus*, the seas were running so high that it looked impossible for anyone to climb aboard. Someone heard the Admiral hail the ship and, realizing that he must be wounded, prepared to lower a chair from the main yardarm. Nelson called for a rope and shouted, "Let me alone! I've got my legs left and one arm." He grabbed the rope and hauled himself aboard ship. Then he said, "Tell the surgeon to get his instruments ready, for I know that I must lose my arm, and the sooner it is off the better."

There was nothing to kill the pain of the operation, for anesthetics had not yet been discovered. While the ship's surgeon cut through the flesh and what was left of the bone, Nelson could only close his eyes and grit his teeth. The surgeon worked fast because he knew that his patient was weak from loss of blood and chilled by his long ride back to the ship from the beach. He cut off Nelson's right arm high above the elbow, tied off the blood vessels and hoped for the best.

The full shock of the injury did not strike Nelson until much later. Within fifteen minutes of the operation he was calling for his flag captain to ask how the battle was going. It was going badly. As one boat after another struggled back to the ship, the sad story was told. Many of the boats had missed the beach and had been dashed to bits on the rocks. Others had made it to the beach, but their troops had been pinned down by the defenders' fire. Even inside the town nearly every street had been commanded by a cannon or fieldpiece. The last few survivors to reach the ships reported that nearly every man who had reached the town had been killed, wounded or forced to surrender. Teneriffe's defenders had been ready and lying in wait for them. Instead of a British assault, the

Teneriffe expedition had turned into a Spanish ambush.

The defeated fleet put out to sea and returned to its base. Then Nelson slowly began to realize how great a personal loss he had suffered. His report of the battle had to be written with his left hand, and it was all he could do to read his own writing. He could not dress himself, and his coat had to be sliced open so the stump of his right arm could fit through. His aides had to cut his food for him when he ate. But most of all he suffered from the never-ending pain. He could still feel the breath-taking agony of the cold steel knife. Nelson's wound healed slowly, and one of the ligatures that had tied off a blood vessel would not come loose. All day and night the wound throbbed. Finally he had no choice but to return to England for recuperation.

Lady Nelson had settled in Bath with Nelson's father, and it was here that Nelson came home on a dusky September night in 1797. He had been at sea more than four years. He strode into the shuttered drawing room with a cheerful hello and a laugh, hoping to soften the shock he knew his appearance would cause. But his forced cheerfulness was not enough. Nelson's wife and father stood stock still as they saw him come through the door.

His body was shrunken into his uniform. His once-blond hair was white. A livid scar creased the right side of his forehead. His right eye was dead and unseeing. And across his chest, almost emphasized by the embroidered decorations of his uniform, was the empty sleeve of his right arm. Here Nelson's wife and father saw, in a way his letters never could tell them, the high price of heroism.

Nelson pretended that he did not notice their reaction. They quickly recovered and tried to join in with his mood of joyous homecoming. After so long an absence he could hardly recognize his young sister; "little Kate" was now nearly a grown lady. His father, though, seemed completely unchanged. And Nelson's wife appeared little aged by her four years of worry. There was much to talk about, once the early awkwardness had passed. But Nelson's joviality wore off as his arm started throbbing again, and that same night the family doctor had to be called in to help change his dressing.

Lady Nelson bravely took a lesson from the doctor on how to care for the wound, but at first she could hardly bear to look at it. And instead of lessening, the pain grew worse. The ligature still would not come free, and an infection built up around it. The stump became hot and swollen, and poultices were applied to soothe it. Almost never did Nelson get a full night's sleep. Sometimes the pain would become so great that in the midst of a journey or a conference he would have to break off and retire to a room by himself, where no one could see him as he sweated out the throbbing agony.

In the hope of finding relief, he and Lady Nelson took lodgings in London, where Nelson was examined by some of England's best surgeons. They considered another operation but could not be sure it would help. They could only advise him that time would tell. So Nelson waited, trying to take his mind off the pain by going to the Admiralty every day. But night after night he lay awake, listening to the city grow quiet around him, counting the hours as they ticked slowly by on his bedroom clock, and finally tossing about in the fitful sleep of fever, which brought no relief at all.

This was also a time for a bit of the glory he had earned. Celebrations were held in his honor. Praise was poured on him by a constant stream of old friends, shipmates and fellow veterans of past campaigns. The Admiralty granted him a pension, for whenever he might retire. The king received him and formally invested him with the title he had won at the Battle of St. Vincent. But perhaps the most rewarding moment came when an old friend, Richard Bulkeley, who had been with Nelson in the San Juan expedition, called on him one evening with his two young sons.

No praise could be more rewarding than the

look in the eyes of the two boys as they studied the great admiral, his uniform embroidered with his honors and medals and his empty sleeve pinned to his blouse. Nelson talked on and on with the boys, telling them about his exploits, describing how he had lost his eye and his arm. And then he brought out his sword.

Young Dick Bulkeley asked if he could hold the sword just for a minute. Sir Horatio slipped it from its scabbard and handed it to him. Standing in the presence of this great man, holding the glittering sword in his hand, young Dick swore that he would someday try to be as great a man as his hero, Admiral Sir Horatio Nelson. The Admiral was to be reminded of this scene a few years later.

Nelson had come home in September. October and most of November passed with no relief from the pain. But then, on the night of November 29, he went to bed and slept soundly until morning, for the first time since the operation aboard his ship four months earlier. When he awoke next morning, relieved and refreshed, he sent for the doctors. They removed the dressing and the ligature came away with it. All pain was gone. The wound was completely recovered.

And within a week Nelson had made formal application to the Admiralty—for sea duty again.

# V I

## BATTLE OF THE NILE: RACE TO EGYPT

 HILE ENGLAND'S HERO OF THE hour was Sir Horatio Nelson, her greatest enemy was a brilliant French general, Napoleon Bonaparte. In the same year that Nelson finally recovered from the amputation of his right arm, Napoleon concluded a brilliant series of military campaigns in Italy and Austria. As a result of these campaigns most of Europe now lay under the control of Napoleon's France. All Englishmen wondered when Napoleon would strike against them. England alone stood in his way. France had an army almost four times the size of England's, and no active enemies to keep it busy on the continent of Europe. This was the time for France to attack England.

But to attack England herself, France had first to subdue England's navy, which protected the island nation. That is why the next seven years saw an extended conflict between the great general of France, Napoleon Bonaparte, and the great admiral of England, Horatio Nelson. From this time on, every major battle Nelson went into was against forces assembled by Napoleon.

The first great battle came after a frustrating three-month chase. Nelson had returned to active duty and was assigned to the Mediterranean. The Admiralty had received the reports it had been expecting and dreading: Napoleon was massing a huge fleet at Toulon, the big French port in the Mediterranean. What was he up to? He could sail out into the Mediterranean and swing in any direction. He could attack England's colonies, her trade routes or even England herself. Somebody had to take a fleet into the enemy waters around Toulon and try to intercept these French ships as they gathered, or at least try to find out what Napoleon was planning. The man selected for the mission was Nelson.

One of England's strongest naval bases is at Gibraltar, at the mouth of the Mediterranean. It is a huge fortress built in towering, solid rock. There Nelson collected a small fleet of fast ships and set out into the Mediterranean, toward Toulon and the massing French fleet.

The reports were beginning to come in now. One of the Admiral's frigates had captured a French corvette. The corvette's men said that the force assembling at Toulon was indeed large: 15 French ships of the line; 400 transport and supply vessels; 40,000 men, including units of the French cavalry that had fought so well on the Continent. And 12,000 of these troops had already embarked. The time was late.

Nelson ordered all sail cracked on, but within hours he had to call for it to be reduced. The fair May weather had turned wet and gusty, and by early morning the *Vanguard* and the rest of the fleet were rolling through a full gale. It was a night of terror. All three of the *Vanguard*'s masts went over the side. Her huge bower anchor began to punch a hole in her side. The lower decks were filling with water. In the black, howling night it was impossible to signal from one ship to another. But when daylight came, another ship in the fleet was able to sail to the *Vanguard*'s aid and take her under tow just as she seemed about to roll over and sink.

Through bow-high seas the *Vanguard* was towed to the nearest port, on the island of Sardinia. What was left of the fleet anchored here for repairs. It was nearly a week before they were ready to sail again, and by this time all of Nelson's small, fast frigates were gone. After they had been battered by the storm, the frigates' senior officer had taken them to Gibraltar. He had seen in the morning that the flagship had lost her masts, and he assumed that Nelson would take the whole fleet back to the main base at Gibraltar for a complete refit.

"I had thought," said Nelson angrily when he heard this, "that the senior officer would have known me better." Nelson would not waste the time for a return to Gibraltar, bad as the damage was. After the hasty repairs at Sardinia, he pushed on for Toulon, hoping that his frigates would find him and rejoin him later.

The frigates never did find him, but some much more important vessels did. As Nelson set out after Napoleon the second time, he was joined by ten British ships of the line, sent out from Gibraltar to help him carry out his orders. The orders were to find Napoleon's fleet and "to take, burn, sink or destroy it."

But when he arrived off Toulon Nelson found that he was too late. Napoleon had sailed. Now the long chase began in earnest.

In came another report: Napoleon had sailed for the Mediterranean island of Malta, at that time ruled by the Knights of Malta. Nelson raced for Malta, to find out that Napoleon had already been there. His troops had quickly forced the surrender of the island, and the French fleet had put out to sea again. To where? Nelson made a guess. The wind had been from the west for the past few days, so a favorable course would be across the Mediterranean to Egypt. This was the gateway to a far greater prize: all the riches of India.

Nelson set his course for Egypt.

One morning, as his fleet raced eastward, a few French frigates were spotted far off on the horizon. But Nelson had no frigates of his own to send after them, and he could not waste time chasing enemy frigates with his big ships of the line. He was sure these could only be enemy dispatch ships, since frigates were normally used for carrying messages and scouting. Nelson estimated that Napoleon's main fleet had nearly a week's head start on him. So he pushed ahead. Little did he realize that on the misty night before he had sailed within a few miles of Napoleon and the entire French fleet. In fact, the French admiral, Francis de Brueys, had heard the British signal guns in the night. Surprised and greatly worried, he turned the whole French fleet northward in order to get out of the way.

The British fleet rushed on. In only six days Nelson sailed 800 miles, nearly two-thirds of the length of the Mediterranean Sea. But when he reached Alexandria, Egypt, he found only a few merchant ships. He did not know, of course, that he had sailed too fast and that Napoleon had been delayed by his slower transports.

Twice the British fleet sailed past the French fleet. They had almost met when the British passed the French a few days earlier. And at Alexandria Nelson's ships had scarcely disappeared to continue their search before the topmasts of

Napoleon's ships could be seen approaching from the west.

For nearly a month Nelson searched the eastern Mediterranean, beyond Alexandria, without finding a trace of Napoleon's fleet. By now his ships badly needed provisions and water. He put back to Sicily. Every report he could get in this area indicated that Napoleon had indeed gone east. Nelson could not understand how he had missed the French fleet, but he decided to make one more search for it. Once again the British fleet sailed east. This time Nelson was sure he would find Napoleon.

And this time the voyage to Alexandria took only four days. As the fleet raced eastward Nelson stepped up the training and made the battle preparations. The fleet sailed in fighting formation, in three divisions. Two would take on the enemy ships of the line while the third division went after the transports. Gun crews went through their paces time after time, until they could fire, reload and fire faster than ever before. New signals were put into the signal books, to take care of any situation that could possibly develop. All Nelson's captains met in *Vanguard*'s cabin for hours of conferences. Every conceivable tactical situation was planned for—if the enemy were at sea or at anchor; if there were a calm or a storm; if it were daylight or darkness. Nelson presented his plans to the captains and asked each for his frank opinion and his own ideas about the coming battle.

Never before in the Royal Navy had this kind of group discussion taken place. The custom had always been for the commander of the fleet simply to announce the plan of battle. His officers carried it out with no questions. These free exchanges between Nelson and his captains produced new and different tactics that were to pay off in the conflict to come. By August 1, 1798, when the towers of Alexandria came into sight once again, the British fleet was battle-ready.

But the enemy was gone.

The scouts sent ahead returned to report that the French fleet had come and sailed away. Napoleon had landed his troops and had already started the military campaign that would conquer most of Egypt.

This was one of the darkest hours in Horatio Nelson's career. He had spent three months chasing Napoleon about the Mediterranean and had been completely outmaneuvered by him. If Nelson had had his frigates for scouting—his "eyes," as he called them—he was sure the French fleet would not have escaped. But whatever the excuse, he had let Napoleon and his fleet get through. Nelson's expedition had been a failure. Ordering his fleet to sail along the coast while he considered what to do next, Nelson went to his cabin for a solemn meal with a few of his officers.

They had barely sat down when they heard the clatter of running steps on the companionway. The officer of the watch raced straight into Nelson's cabin to say: "Sir, a signal is just now made. The enemy is in Aboukir Bay."

Nelson reached the quarterdeck in seconds, to see in the distance the signal flags flying from the *Goliath*, one of his lead ships. Her masthead lookout had spotted, in Aboukir Bay, only fifteen miles east of Alexandria, the masts of what looked like sixteen warships sitting at anchor. He barely had time to report his find when the news was also shouted by the lookouts of the *Goliath*'s consort, the *Zealous*. Now, as the signal flags fluttered in the breeze, the sound of cheers welled up throughout the fleet. The long chase was over.

Nelson ordered the signal flag hoisted: *Prepare for battle*. Then, with his first satisfied smile in three months, he went below and ordered the dinner which had been interrupted. He knew that it would be an hour or more before they reached Aboukir Bay. He knew that it would be some time before he could enjoy a leisurely meal in peace again. He also knew that this meal might be his last.

Admiral Francis de Brueys of the French navy was certain that he was in a perfect position for defense. He had landed Napoleon and his troops and had taken his ships of the line and frigates on to this anchorage. Aboukir Bay is one of the two places where the River Nile flows into the Mediterranean. The bay is a mass of shoals, and in 1798 few charts of the bay had ever been made. De Brueys had taken soundings of the depth of the water and had lined his ships up along the shore, as close as he could get to the shallow water along the beach. In a line like this he commanded the approach to his anchorage, with row upon row of guns presented broadside to any ship that tried to come near. Since he was too close to the shore for anyone to get inside his line, he could double the strength of his gun crews on the outward side of each ship. And to add to his defensive power he had mounted cannon on an island near by.

De Brueys knew that a defensive position almost exactly like this had worked before. During the American Revolution a British admiral had anchored his ships this way in the West Indies and had beaten off a fleet three times the size of his own. De Brueys had 13 ships of the line and 4 frigates, mounting 1,196 guns, and 11,230 men. This was a huge fleet for the Mediterranean, and he doubted that the enemy's was as large.

So when he first received the report, "Enemy in sight," the French admiral refused to become as excited as he had earlier when he had heard the signal guns in the middle of the Mediterranean. This time he was ready for the British fleet. Aboukir Bay would be difficult enough to enter in broad daylight, with the sounding lead measuring the depth all the way. It was now late in the afternoon, and de Brueys did not see how the British could attack before darkness. He was sure they would not try to attack after sunset. If they were so foolish as to risk it, he could smash every ship that did not go aground, one by one as they came into range of his broadsides. No, he was sure the British would wait outside the bay for him to come out in the morning. That he would be glad to do, since he could already see that the enemy's force was smaller than his. His big flagship, the *Orient*, carried 120 guns, almost twice the number of the largest British ship. He had thirteen ships of the line, and he could make out only ten enemy ships approaching the bay. De Brueys called his officers together to plan strategy for the morning. But he was in no hurry, and he did not even bother to recall the sailors who were ashore collecting wood and water.

The Admiral's mistake was in assuming that his attacker would employ normal tactics. He had no way of knowing that the commander of the fleet coming toward him was Admiral Sir Horatio Nelson. And he had no way of knowing that Nelson had already planned one step ahead of him.

Nelson had put himself in the place of the French admiral and had reached the same conclusion: if he waited until morning, he would face a superior force in a pitched battle. And if the French admiral expected him to wait until morning because of the difficulties of attacking at night, the obvious thing to do was to attack at once and catch him unprepared.

At this point three of Nelson's ships of the line had not caught up to him. One, the *Culloden*, was delayed because she had a captured ship under tow. The other two, the *Alexander* and the *Swiftsure*, were still racing to catch up with the fleet after their scouting run into Alexandria Harbor. These difficulties could be made up for by the fact that the attack would be unexpected and he would catch the enemy off guard.

Nelson explained his strategy to Captain Edward Berry, who said excitedly, "If we succeed, what will the world say?" Nelson replied, "There is no *if* in the case. That we shall succeed is certain. Who may live to tell the story is a very different question."

As the fleet ran down toward the shore, Nelson studied Aboukir Bay. A forest of masts rose above the sand banks at the entrance. On deck just above his stern window two sailors were also looking at the bay. "There they are, Jack," said one. "If we don't beat them, they'll beat us."

Nelson turned to an aide and gave the order: "Signal all ships to form the line of battle. We are going in after them."

# VII

## BATTLE OF THE NILE: NIGHT OF FIRE

 LOWLY, SOUNDING WITH THE LEAD line as they came, the fleet crept into Aboukir Bay toward the waiting French warships. The soundings showed fifteen fathoms, then thirteen, then eleven, then ten. Near Nelson's *Vanguard* was the British *Zealous*, still in the lead. As they rounded what looked like a shoal at the entrance, Nelson hailed her captain, Samuel Hood. Did his soundings indicate that they could swing in toward the center of the bay? Hood replied: "If you will allow me the honor of leading you into battle, I will keep the lead going."

Nelson said, "You have my leave, and I wish you success." He raised his hat in salute.

Hood raised his and the freshening breeze snatched it away. To a lieutenant chasing after it, Hood called, "Never mind, Webley! There it goes for luck. Put the helm up and make sail!"

It was 5:40 P.M. Another signal flag rose to the *Vanguard's* masthead: *Prepare for close action.* Picking up speed as they loosed more sails to the breeze, the British fleet glided into battle order. And as the ships came into range, the French gunners launched the Battle of the Nile.

The French tricolor rose and, at the signal, the massive line of guns opened fire. Cannonballs, shells and jagged shot ripped through the British rigging. Men loosing and furling sail were toppled from the yardarms. Along the deck the shower of shot and flying splinters mowed down anyone who did not—or could not—crouch behind some shelter. In the next few minutes every man stationed at the forward six guns was killed or wounded.

But the British did not fire back, yet. They came straight on, each captain keeping exactly to his course. A small French ship ducked out of the formation and tried to lure the British ships across the bay onto a shoal. No British captain paid any attention; each sailed on toward his battle position. Here at last the long hours of training and conferences were paying off. One British ship, the *Culloden*, went aground off Aboukir island. She had been hastening to join the rest of the fleet after getting rid of the captured ship she was towing. Her signals immediately warned the others away from the shoal. Only the *Leander* stayed behind to try to help her.

As the British line came into the bay, the ships

split off. And at this point the French admiral realized, too late, how Nelson had outsmarted him.

Admiral de Brueys had assumed that if the British did attempt to attack the French fleet at anchor, the British ships would have to sail along the line of anchored French warships. The battle would consist of an exchange of broadsides between two lines of ships. And in such a battle the heavier weight of French fire power could be expected to win. Not only did the French have more guns, but they had two crews for every gun. De Brueys thought he had anchored his ships too close to the shore for the British to slip between him and the beach, so his inshore guns and gun crews would not be needed. But that was the very point in which de Brueys had underestimated the tactical genius of his rival commander.

Nelson had no intention of getting into such a line-to-line battle. One reason he wanted to attack while the French were at anchor was so he could concentrate his entire fleet on part of the French fleet instead of all of it. De Brueys had assumed that any such maneuvering would be impossible in a bay so full of shoals. Nelson, however, had realized that any ship rides back on her anchor line. Therefore each French ship must have floated back as her anchor line ran out. So there must be just enough water to permit ships of the British line to squeeze between the French ships and the shore. And that was where the five lead-

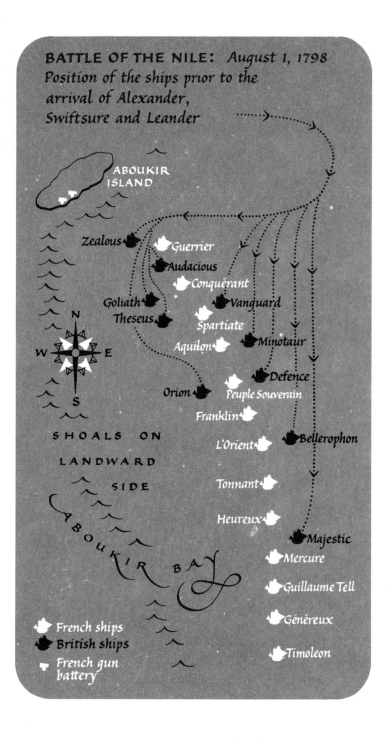

BATTLE OF THE NILE: August 1, 1798
Position of the ships prior to the
arrival of Alexander,
Swiftsure and Leander

ABOUKIR
ISLAND

Zealous

Guerrier

Audacious

Conquérant

Goliath

Vanguard

Theseus

Spartiate

N
W E
S

Aquilon

Minotaur

Defence

Orion

Peuple Souverain

Franklin

SHOALS ON

Bellerophon

LANDWARD

L'Orient

SIDE

Tonnant

ABOUKIR BAY

Heureux

Majestic

Mercure

Guillaume Tell

Généreux

French ships
British ships
French gun
battery

Timoleon

ing British ships now set their course. After they were anchored on the landward side of the first six ships of the French line, the other half of the British fleet steered for the seaward side of the enemy line. Once the British vessels had swung into position, the foremost section of the French fleet suddenly found itself surrounded.

The rest of the British anchors went down. All sails were furled tight and hard and drenched with water to keep them from catching fire. And then, as darkness began to settle over Aboukir Bay, the British finally opened fire.

Immediately Nelson's tactics began to pay off. He had guessed correctly that the French had prepared to fight only with their seaward guns. Most of those on the landward side were not readied, and much of the gear cleared away from the seaward guns was stacked up in the way of those on the landward side. As the French gun crews tried desperately to clear their inshore guns, the broadsides from the British cut them to pieces. Great murderous splinters from the piled-up tables and furniture flew across the enemy decks.

Firing almost unopposed, the British ships near the shore pounded the French ships to wreckage. The lead ship in the French line, the *Guerrier*, was dismasted in twelve minutes. Another was soon battered into helplessness. Within two hours the first five ships in the French line were out of action, and Nelson was already planning his next step: to move down the line and take on the center of the enemy fleet. He was standing on the quarterdeck of the *Vanguard* with Captain Edward Berry, studying a crude map of the bay, when he was hit.

Among the types of ammunition used by gun crews in those days was langridge, a bundle of jagged scrap metal which flew through the air like so many knives when fired from a ship's cannon. It was particularly useful for cutting up sails and rigging, and the French were employing it to good effect. It was a piece of langridge which caught Nelson in the head.

The metal struck him on the forehead and cut through to the bone. Blood poured down his face and chest. The torn flesh fell over his good eye and blinded him. He fell to the deck, but was quickly caught up in the arms of Captain Berry, who summoned help to carry him below.

In the *Vanguard*'s cockpit, deep in the ship below the waterline, the surgeon was at work tending the more than seventy men who had been wounded. Immediately he turned his attention to the Admiral, but Nelson refused. "No," he said, "I will take my turn."

While Nelson waited he could hear, above the moans and cries of the wounded around him, the rumble and thud of gun carriages on the decks overhead, the blasting of the broadsides, and the cheers as one of her volleys scored a hit. He also heard the thump of enemy cannonballs hitting the *Vanguard*'s side.

When the surgeon finally got to Nelson, he announced happily that the injury was nothing more than a deep flesh wound. The good eye did not seem to be affected. But both eyes had to be covered up by the bandage. The blindfolded admiral was then led to a cot in the room where the ship's bread was stored, and told to rest.

Nelson promptly called for his secretary, to dictate the news of the victory which he could now send to England. The secretary, who had been wounded himself, took one look at the pale, bandaged admiral and became so flustered that he could not take down the message. Nelson called for another aide. The new one found that the Admiral had pushed the bandage up off his good eye and was himself scrawling with his left hand: "Almighty God has blessed His Majesty's arms in the late battle . . ."

At this point Captain Berry arrived to announce that the huge French flagship, the 120-gun *Orient*, was on fire. Nelson jumped up and climbed the companionway steps to the quarterdeck.

Aboukir Bay was an inferno. It echoed with the boom and smash of broadsides. The hot, black night lit up with flashes of gunfire. On one ship there was a sudden roaring flash as a sail caught fire. On another a steadier crackling fire marked the burning of a mast and rigging. With a groaning crash another mast toppled, like a falling tree, over the side and into the water, amid a tangle of rigging and a flurry of canvas. The water around the fleets cascaded with the splash of cannonballs and hissed as burning spars plunged into the sea. Debris and the heads of swimming sailors bobbed on top of the waves. Over all lay a murky, yellowish cloud from which a light ash drifted down onto everything below.

One steady, mounting glare was beginning to light the entire bay. It came from the French flagship *Orient*. The *Orient*'s crew had been painting her during the afternoon, little dreaming that she might be fighting for her life that night. Now the paint and oil caught fire, turning the ship into one big torch. The main part of the fire was near the flagship's stern, and in its light Nelson could see the bucket brigades trying to put it out. The French had good reason for wanting to save the *Orient*. Not only was she the greatest ship of the French navy, but she carried in her hold £600,000 in gold and diamonds, which were to pay for Napoleon's campaign in the Middle East.

As the *Orient*'s crew tried to fight the fire, British crews trained their guns on the ship to keep the fire fighters away. The flames raced up the rigging and spread along the new paint on the ship's sides. In the dancing light men could be seen jumping over the rail, to swim to safety before the fire reached the ship's powder magazine. Some of the *Orient*'s guns kept firing, but gradually the only sound was the crackling of the fire as it spread throughout the ship. And, one by one, the British attackers closest to her slipped their cables to move away from the explosion that would come when the fire reached the ship's huge store of gunpowder.

As the *Orient* burned, every ship in the bay was illuminated by the wavering light. Looking about him, his bandage still pulled up, Nelson could see that victory was only a matter of time. He asked if the *Vanguard* had any serviceable boats left. There was one. Nelson ordered it sent over to the *Orient*, to save as many enemy lives as possible.

The British ships whose arrival had been delayed now came into the battle. Two of them aimed their broadsides at the burning *Orient*. Nelson made ready to move down to the end of the French line and finish off the rest of the enemy fleet. A few ships at the end of the French line were preparing for a desperate race to escape to the open sea. Then the *Orient* blew up.

The explosion was so great that it startled French troops at Rosetta, ten miles away. Gun crews on the lower decks of nearly every vessel in the bay thought some part of their own ships had exploded. After the awesome eruption there was silence for nearly ten minutes, a silence broken only by the rain of sparks, red-hot ammunition and burning spars and debris all over the bay. Then, as if both sides had paused for breath, the battle raged on.

But it was now certain that the French were beaten. By 3:00 A.M. the defenders' fire had become sporadic, and Nelson was finally persuaded to go to bed. He was up at dawn to look at the aftermath of the Battle of the Nile.

His first order was for every British ship to hold religious services on deck, to offer thanksgiving to God for the great victory granted them. The services were held in a scene of utter desolation. From shore to shore Aboukir Bay was a floating mass of charred and twisted wreckage. On some hulks a few fires continued to burn, and the yellowish pall of smoke still hung over the bay. Barrels, broken spars, splintered masts and corpses washed back and forth with the tide. It would take more than a day just to bury the dead. Where the great French flagship *Orient* had been there were now only a few jagged timbers sticking out of the shallow water. The *Orient* had had a crew of more than 1,000; after the explosion the British boats had been able to rescue only 70. Nearly all the rest, including Admiral de Brueys, had gone down with the ship.

Nelson estimated that 1,400 Frenchmen were killed and 600 wounded; 218 British died and 677 were wounded. More than 3,000 French officers and sailors were taken prisoner, most of whom Nelson sent ashore so Napoleon's forces in Egypt could care for the wounded. Of the thirteen French ships of the line, nine had surrendered and two had burned to the water's edge. Only two had managed to slip out of the bay, because there were no British ships in good condition to chase them. One that escaped was the *Guillaume Tell*, carrying French Rear Admiral Pierre Villeneuve.

Admiral Villeneuve would live to fight Nelson another day, but he was one of the very few. In the Battle of the Nile Sir Horatio Nelson utterly smashed the French fleet. His victory was described as England's greatest since the defeat of the Spanish Armada. In some ways it was greater because, although every British ship was damaged, not one was lost.

The entire Mediterranean Sea was now under British control. Throughout Europe, countries that had leaned toward all-powerful France began to favor England. Most important, Nelson's capture of the French fleet left Napoleon Bonaparte trapped in the Middle East. The British navy quickly put a blockade around Alexandria and the nearby ports, to make sure he stayed there. France felt his loss as soon as some of her conquered countries rose against her. The same soldiers who had swept through Austria and part of Italy were now driven back toward France. Suddenly, and almost entirely because of Nelson's great victory at the Nile, France began to lose the control she had won over Europe.

When the news of the Nile reached home, England went wild. Nelson's title was immediately raised: Sir Horatio Nelson became Lord Nelson of the Nile and Burnham Thorpe, with a pension of £2,000 a year. Celebrations were held throughout the country. Nelson's face appeared on cups and plates, banners and inn signs, in memory of the historic victory. At Naples, where he brought his fleet for repairs and where he hoped to recover from a fever brought on by his wound, the bay was speckled by the sails of 500 pleasure boats that came out to welcome him. Naples' King Ferdinand IV was rowed out to the *Vanguard* in his golden galley to hail Nelson as Italy's "Deliverer and Preserver." On the wharves an orchestra from the opera house played "Rule Britannia" as Nelson stepped ashore. On the Naples hillsides houses were hung with flags and bunting, and Neapolitans greeted him by holding bird cages in the air and releasing the birds as he passed by. And during his long recuperation at Naples, Nelson was given an Italian title: Duke of Brontë. Ever afterward he signed his name "Nelson and Brontë."

It was more than a year before Nelson recovered fully from his wound and returned to England.

With him were his close friends, Sir William Hamilton, British Ambassador to Naples, and Lady Hamilton. England had not forgotten him. The British gave him a hero's homecoming. At Yarmouth, where he landed, the townspeople took the horses from the traces and pulled his carriage through the streets as the crowds lined his way and cheered him. At the inn where he stayed the landlady asked his permission to change the inn's name to "The Nelson Arms." Nelson laughed and replied, "That would be absurd, seeing that I have but one." As he entered church on Sunday the congregation rose and the organ broke out with the strains of "See, the Conquering Hero Comes." In other towns people carried him about on their shoulders. Lord Nelson had achieved in full measure the promise young Horatio Nelson had made to himself on that afternoon a quarter of a century earlier in the cabin of the *Dolphin.*

But Nelson's struggle with Napoleon was far from finished. Only a year after the Battle of the Nile a French frigate slipped through the British Mediterranean blockade and carried Napoleon back to France. He landed there on October 8, 1799. Napoleon had been France's greatest general. Now he became her First Consul. And he set out to conquer England with an entirely new strategy of war.

# VIII

## BATTLE OF COPENHAGEN: THE BOLD GAMBLE

APOLEON BONAPARTE WAS STILL convinced that the only thing standing between him and the conquest of all Europe was the British navy. After the Battle of the Nile he realized that the French navy alone could not beat the British navy, so he went to work to form a coalition. With promises, treaties—and threats—he started lining up the governments of other countries behind that of France. Denmark, Sweden, Prussia and Russia joined the alliance. England's leaders watched with alarm. If these nations really joined together their navies, they could assemble 123 ships of the line and more than 160 smaller vessels—a far larger force than England had ever faced. England's prime minister decided that he must move fast. Before the alliance could be formed into one huge force, its parts must be attacked singly.

So in March of 1801, Horatio Nelson found himself ordered to sea once again. The enemy this time was the Danish navy, which could become the strongest member of the alliance if it were not checked. The British force included eighteen ships of the line and frigates, sloops, brigs and cutters to a total of fifty-three vessels.

The British fleet had two missions. The first was to meet with the Danish government officials and try to reach an agreement not to fight against each other. British diplomats sailed with the fleet to handle these negotiations. The commander of the fleet was Admiral Sir Hyde Parker, better known as a diplomat than as a fighting admiral. But if diplomacy failed, the British navy was to fight. That was what Nelson, the fighting admiral, was there for. Because of the diplomatic mission of the fleet Nelson was officially second in command.

After the warm, blue waters of the Mediterranean, the voyage through the gray, white-capped waters of the North Sea was a shock. As the ships plunged northward, snow drifted through to the lower decks. Sleet covered the yardarms, and the rigging clacked with ice. One after another the men came down with colds and pneumonia. Half the crew was sick by the time a low-lying stretch of land appeared through a shower of snowflakes. This was the Skaw, the northern point of Jutland, and here the fleet anchored.

Under a flag of truce the diplomats went ashore. For days they argued with the Danes, while Nelson stayed on his ship and fretted. He was already certain that the diplomats would get nowhere while the British fleet stayed out of sight. "A Danish minister," he said, "would think twice before he put his name to war with England, when the next moment he would probably see his master's fleet in flames. The Dane should see our flag waving every moment he lifted up his head." Nelson knew that the longer the Danes could keep the diplomats arguing, the more time they had to prepare their defenses. So he was not surprised when the British diplomats came back to the flagship and sadly announced that the Danes refused to agree. In fact, they had strengthened their positions until the Danish navy looked unbeatable.

Nelson had urged that the diplomats scout the Danes' defenses before they returned to the British fleet. The reports they brought back made the British commander, Sir Hyde Parker, hesitate to carry out the fleet's second mission: attack. The Danish Fleet was anchored in line just as de Brueys had anchored his French Fleet at the Nile. But this time there was no room between the anchored ships and the shore. The Danish ships were brought up almost against the walls of the city. Not only that, the entire shore front of the city was bristling with guns, aimed to fire over the Danish ships at any attacker. The Danish ships alone, not counting the batteries on the shore, amounted to more than the entire British force; and they mounted 634 guns.

Sir Hyde Parker was dismayed by these reports. It was clear to him that the chances for a British victory at this point were poor. In the council of war held in his cabin he considered turning away and not rushing blindly into what seemed to him a certain defeat. This was where the fighting admiral came in.

Nelson used the same reasoning he had employed on the afternoon when he had been approaching the Nile. The enemy looked strong indeed, but the longer the British waited, the stronger the enemy's position would be. While the British fleet had sat off the Skaw, the Danes had already strengthened their defenses. Give them more time and they would grow stronger yet. Why had the British sailed through the ice and storms of the North Sea? To smash the Danish navy before it was joined by the navies of Sweden and Russia. By then it really might be too late, but it was not too late now.

"Not a moment should be lost," Nelson argued, "in attacking the enemy. They will every day and every hour be stronger; we shall never be so good a match for them as at this very moment."

Then he turned to another argument, the one that was all-important in his eyes. "Here you are," he reminded his commander, "with almost the safety, certainly with the honor, of England more entrusted to you than ever yet fell to the lot of any British officer. On your decision depends whether our country shall be degraded in the eyes of Europe, or whether she shall rear her head higher than ever. . . . The boldest measures are the safest."

Nelson capped his argument by volunteering to sail into Copenhagen Harbor with only half of the British fleet. Give me ten ships of the line, he said, and I can do it. Sir Hyde Parker was a cautious, perhaps even timid, man. But he was not a coward. Against such arguments he could not hold out. He turned the command of the attack over to Nelson, and promised him not ten but twelve ships of the line.

Copenhagen Harbor is long and narrow. In order to approach it the British ships had to sail in past a mud bank called Middle Ground and then turn in the opposite direction to go on into the inner harbor. During the time spent on diplomatic negotiations, the Danes had removed all the buoys marking the channel into the harbor. Nelson ordered new soundings made and new buoys put down. And on the wild, windy night before he launched his attack, he took a small boat and sailed twenty miles amongst ice floes through the long, winding approaches to the harbor, overseeing the job himself.

With the morning's light, his attack force weighed anchor and sailed slowly past Middle Ground on a favorable wind. When the ships dropped their anchors again that evening, they could look into the inner harbor and see the great long row of Danish ships of the line. The Danish shore batteries towered above them.

As darkness fell and the shapes of the Danish ships faded, only the lights of the enemy blinked across the water. Nelson called his captains together for a council of war. In the soft yellow lantern light of his cabin he went over the plan of action for each ship. This was not like the briefing before the Battle of the Nile. Then every captain had been able to devote long hours and days to learning and discussing his part in the action. This time Nelson had not been able to rehearse his officers, so all the preparations had to be understood in this one meeting on the eve of the battle. Each man, as he looked about the low-ceilinged cabin, could try to guess which of his fellow officers would be alive at the same time tomorrow. Each man knew that he was going in against a larger and more heavily armed force than his own. And each captain was given his own special orders for his own special part in the battle to come.

But Nelson felt none of the dread that must

have hung heavily on the hearts of his captains. He raised his glass to toast a fair wind with the dawn. And so eagerly did he go over the tactics for each ship that, when his captains returned to their cabins, they too seemed to be excited by the coming battle and anxious to get into action.

Because they would be up at dawn, Nelson ended the council of war at nine o'clock that evening. But he called the ships' clerks together and ordered the battle plans written down for each captain. The clerks worked through the night. Such orders had to be written by hand so a copying project like this normally took a day or two. While the clerks worked through the night, Nelson's aides reminded him that he had had scarcely any sleep in the past week. He had spent the previous night out on the cold, black waters of the outer harbor, supervising the placement of the buoys. Nelson finally agreed to lie down on a cot that was brought for him.

He soon got up to greet Captain Sir Thomas Hardy, who had sneaked up near the enemy in the dark to measure the water near the anchored ships. Hardy reported that he had slipped right under the bow of the leading enemy ship, so close that he had taken his soundings with a pole in order not to be heard. There was plenty of water alongside, he reported. Nelson thanked him and returned to his cot. But throughout the night he kept calling for an aide or a clerk to make a

change or improve the orders for the battle. It was six o'clock in the morning before the last order was completed. By that time Nelson had already finished breakfast.

The wind had changed. This was unexpected luck, but it was good luck for Nelson only because he had worked through the night to prepare for it. Another admiral might not have pushed his aides and clerks through the night to have the orders finished and the battle preparations made. But now, as the wind changed for Nelson, the plan of battle was in each captain's cabin, and each crew was at its gun. The British fleet was ready.

It was 9:30 on the morning of April 2, 1801, when the attack force weighed anchor and swung into line. The sky was cloudy and the breeze was just enough to move each ship along as her anchor splashed out of the water and her sails filled. The lead ship was the *Edgar*, the only one with a pilot who knew the waters of the harbor. Aboard the *Edgar* no one spoke. Only the chanted commands of the pilot and the helmsman could be heard as the ship moved slowly toward the inner harbor and the bristling line of guns.

At the other end of Middle Ground Sir Hyde Parker could only watch. His plan was to follow up Nelson's attack with an approach from the opposite side, but he was held back by the same wind that was carrying Nelson's ships into the

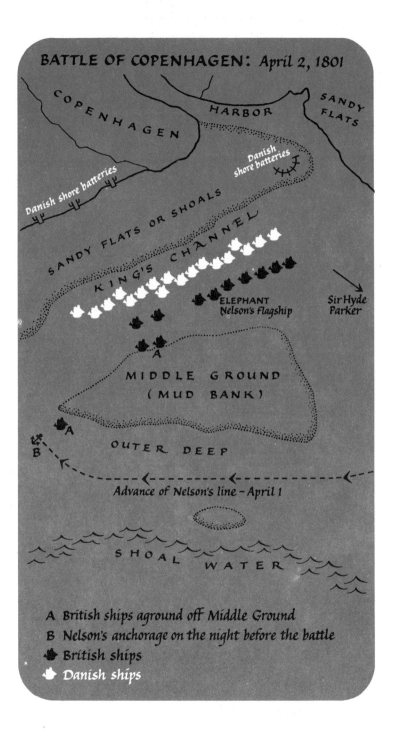

inner harbor. The Danes must have been surprised to see this small force moving slowly but surely down toward their powerful line of defense.

Nelson did not plan to take on a few ships at a time, as he had at the Battle of the Nile. He realized that this battle could only be a slugging match and that it could go on for hours. As he wrote later, "Here was no maneuvering. It was downright fighting." If he tried to break it into separate engagements, he would only tire his gun crews. There was no room for maneuvering or cutting the enemy's line or attacking him from two sides. It had to be a simple, classic broadside-to-broadside battle, and the fleet that threw the most shot and shell would win. So Nelson ordered his captains to sail straight down the Danish line, firing as they went.

The lead ship rode safely into the harbor; but then one, two and three of the British line suddenly came to a halt. They were fast aground on the edge of Middle Ground. Nelson was in a following ship, but he managed to swing out and around the nearest ship aground. The rest of his force followed. Nelson now had nine ships of the line instead of twelve, against the Danes' eighteen. But he held his course, straight for the long row of Danish ships and the glowering shore batteries beyond.

It was 10:05 when the first shot was fired—a crashing broadside from the head of the Danish line as the first of the British attackers glided by. Within minutes the two fleets were exchanging broadsides. Within an hour Nelson's force was alongside the Danish line, and the harbor rocked with the thunder of the Battle of Copenhagen.

Now the long days and nights of gun drill began to pay off. The enemy had nearly two guns for every one of Nelson's. Yet the British began immediately to do more damage to the Danish ships than the Danes could do to them. All along the Danish line, holes began to appear in the ships' sides. Masts split and tumbled into the water and fires flared on the decks. But right away Nelson noticed an ominous sign: small boats were coming out from the shore batteries to the Danish ships, bringing replacements for the gun crews. When a Danish gun went silent, it soon opened up again as a fresh crew from land took over. So the battle roared on, hour after hour, as more and more reinforcements poured from the mainland onto the Danish ships.

From his vantage point at the other end of the mud flats, still waiting for a favorable slant of wind, Sir Hyde Parker watched in alarm. He could see that one-fourth of Nelson's force had run aground. He could see the tremendous power of the Danes' fire. And he could see the unending line of boats ferrying recruits from the city to the ships. By the time the battle had gone on for two and a half hours, Sir Hyde concluded that it was hopeless. Not even Nelson could hold out against a limitless force like this. His gun crews still fired faster and with better aim. But they could not keep it up forever. Sir Hyde also knew that Nelson would never quit on his own accord; he would fight on to the death. The only way to break off this losing battle was to order Nelson to retreat. Sir Hyde watched for a while longer and then unhappily gave the order: *Hoist number 39.* This was the signal for recall.

Aboard Nelson's ship the air screamed with ball and scatter shot. Wood splinters the size of spears ripped across the deck. A yellowish cloud kept nearly everyone coughing. It was almost impossible to shout above the din. Nelson was striding back and forth across the quarterdeck, as he always did when the battle was joined and the final outcome depended on the gun crews. He paused in his pacing as a ball struck the mainmast and filled the air with huge, whirring splinters. Turning to an aide beside him, Nelson shouted into his ear, "It is warm work. This day may be the last to any of us at a moment." He took up his pacing again, then stopped to add, "But mark you, I wouldn't be elsewhere for thousands."

It was at this point that the signal officer gave a shout. Sir Hyde's flagship had hoisted number 39.

Nelson paused for a second, then resumed his stride. The signal officer watched him walk forward a few paces, turn and walk aft. The officer then went over to meet the Admiral as he turned again, and repeated the message in a louder voice, above the noise of the firing. Should he hoist 39 for Nelson's fleet?

"No," said Nelson.

He resumed his stride, a thoughtful frown on his face. His aide continued to walk beside him, disturbed and puzzled by the signal and Nelson's reaction to it.

Nelson stopped and turned to his aide again. "Do you know what is shown aboard the commander in chief?" he asked. "To leave off action!" He paused. "Leave off action!" he repeated. Then a sly smile crossed his face. "You know," he said, "I have only one eye. I have a right to be blind sometimes." He raised his telescope to his blind right eye, lowered it and said, "I do not really see the signal." He called to the signal officer: "Keep mine for closer battle flying. Nail it to the mast!"

Nelson had taken a bold gamble. If he failed now, his career was ended. But he had already sensed that he would not fail. He had noticed something that his commander, many miles away, could not: the enemy's fire was slackening.

It took an expert eye and ear to notice it. But on one Danish ship a gun went silent and was

not put into action **again**. On another a fire spread because there were not enough men to put it out. And then the first Danish flag came fluttering down.

Nelson sent a boat to accept the ship's surrender. As the boat neared the prize, the ship's guns opened up again. This happened a second and a third time. Soon one Danish ship after another was signaling that its crew had had enough. But as the British captors tried to board, they rowed into a curtain of fire.

To Nelson this was inexcusable. Never in his

career had he seen a ship open fire once her flag had been struck. He may not have guessed what was happening: the landsmen who were being ferried out to the ships did not know the cardinal rule of naval warfare, that a surrendered ship cannot open fire again. In any case, Nelson determined to put a stop to this kind of fighting immediately.

Calling for his aide, he dictated a message to the enemy:

TO THE BROTHERS OF ENGLISHMEN, THE DANES

Lord Nelson has direction to spare Denmark, when no longer resisting; but if the firing is continued on the part of Denmark, Lord Nelson will be obliged to set on fire all the floating-batteries he has taken, without having the power of saving the brave Danes who have defended them. . . .

*Nelson and Brontë, Vice Admiral under the command of Sir Hyde Parker*

Under a flag of truce this letter was sent ashore. Denmark's Prince Regent was at the water front commanding the Danish defense. He read the letter and realized that it was fair warning: either his fleet must surrender, or Nelson would send fire ships down on the remaining vessels. Many thousands of Danish sailors would die in what was by now a hopeless cause. The Prince ordered the white flag of truce to be hoisted over the area. The Battle of Copenhagen was over.

There remained the tasks of rounding up the prizes, treating the wounded, burying the dead and negotiating surrender terms with the Prince. More than 250 British had been killed and nearly 700 wounded. But the Danes had paid a higher price: nearly 800 killed and more than 900 wounded, with 2,000 taken prisoner. Nelson went ashore to meet the Prince and talk terms. When they had reached agreement, Nelson paid his respects to the bravery of the Danes. He had been in more than 100 battles, he said, but this was the hardest fought of all. "The French," he told Denmark's Prince, "fought bravely; but they could not have stood for one hour the fight which the Danes supported for four." He was introduced to one of the young officers who had led the Danish defense. This man, Lord Nelson told the Prince, should be made an admiral.

"If, my lord," the Prince replied, "I am to make all my brave officers admirals, I should have no captains or lieutenants in my service."

The victory at Copenhagen was also recognized by the British commander. When the battle ended,

Nelson said to his aide, only half joking, "Well, I have fought contrary to orders, and I shall perhaps be hanged." But when he went aboard Sir Hyde Parker's flagship, he was greeted with congratulations. Sir Hyde realized that he was the one who had been mistaken.

When the news of Copenhagen reached England, the Admiralty responded with new orders to the Baltic Fleet. Sir Hyde Parker was ordered home, and Lord Nelson was placed in command.

On the day that Nelson received the news, the fleet immediately weighed anchor and sailed out to search for the other two navies in the alliance, those of Sweden and Russia. But Nelson had already written home, "We shall not have to fire again in the Baltic." And he was right. The strength of the alliance had been broken.

One further result of Copenhagen was Nelson's elevation to the title of viscount. As he went ashore on his return home, the crowds hailed him and cheered him as never before. His first act, before taking part in any of the celebrations, was to call at the hospital at Yarmouth, to visit the men who had been wounded at Copenhagen. Then he joined in the parades, attended the banquets and accepted the honors, after which he went home.

He well deserved his rest, and England cheered him with good reason. At the Battle of Copenhagen he had once again thwarted the world-conquering

ambitions of Napoleon Bonaparte. He was now the hero not only of England but of the entire world that feared Napoleon. But Nelson, and England, would need to rest and gather strength. For Napoleon had one more plan—this one the most desperate of all. Napoleon determined to launch a direct, all-out attack on England herself. And he knew that it would have to be done with an overwhelming force.

# I X

## A DEADLY GAME OF TAG

HILE NAPOLEON PAINSTAKINGLY prepared his great invasion, England relaxed. In accordance with the terms of The Treaty of Amiens, a truce signed in 1802, half of the British army was sent home. More than sixty of the Royal Navy's ships were put in storage or sold off, and more than forty thousand seamen were let go. Arms, ammunition and other equipment that had been left over from the battles of the Nile and Copenhagen were sold to the highest bidder. Often the highest bidder happened to be an agent from France.

Meanwhile France slowly built up her army and navy. Thousands of troops were billeted along the coast of France, right across the Channel from England. Everywhere in France, shipyards worked day and night, building flat-bottomed barges that could cross the Channel and land on England's beaches. The shipyards also rushed work on frigates and ships of the line, so Napoleon could build up a huge French fleet.

His plan was to pour his army across the Channel in one overwhelming wave. To do this, he explained to his admirals, he needed to wrest control of the Channel away from the British navy for only a few hours. Once his army had landed in England, he was certain that he could march across country to London and capture the capital. Then England would be his, and France would be undisputed ruler of all Europe. If the French navy could hold off or lure away the British navy just for those few hours, Europe would be his.

Gradually the French force grew. British travelers returned home from France, reporting on the thousands of soldiers they had seen along the Channel coastline. Other reports told the British Admiralty of a great French fleet massing at Toulon, France's big port in the Mediterranean Sea. So the Admiralty turned to the only man they felt could take on such a fleet.

Horatio Nelson was at his new home in Merton, near London. He was enjoying his first long rest ashore since the time he had recuperated from the loss of his arm. Now he received warning that war was about to break out again. And on May 18, 1803, England did declare war on France. That same day, at 4:00 A.M., Nelson left Merton to report back for duty.

A Deadly Game of Tag

Waiting for him was the *Victory*. Almost half a block long, her masts taller than a fifteen-story building, the *Victory* was one of the greatest ships of the line in the Royal Navy. She had 3 decks of cannon, 110 guns in all, and she carried a crew of 840 men. Setting forth in a driving rainstorm, Nelson took the *Victory* racing down to the Mediterranean. There he gathered a task force and set his course for the waters off Toulon.

The French fleet was still in the port, loading supplies, recruiting men and bending on sails. Nelson ordered his fleet to cruise back and forth off the harbor, and settled back to wait for the French to come out and fight. But the French would not come out. Days became weeks, and weeks became months, and still Nelson waited. Winter came, and howling northwesters swept down from the Alps and across the Gulf of Lyon. The ships' rigging rotted and broke, and sails and masts went over the side in the storms. The hulls strained and warped. By spring the ships' bottoms were coated with barnacles and trailed long tails of seaweed which slowed them so much that some vessels could not even tack to windward. Summer brought some relief, but not to Nelson himself. His remaining eye began to grow dim from the strain of the hours on deck, forever looking through his telescope across the glare of the Mediterranean. The *Victory*'s doctors tried to make him wear a green eyeshade, but it was little help.

§ 109 §

The long watch also wore on the nerves of the crews. Nelson tried to ease their life. He saw to it that fresh provisions were brought out from Gibraltar, the nearest British naval base. There were oranges and lemons to prevent scurvy. Nelson liked to remind the Admiralty that "it is easier for an officer to keep men healthy than for a physician to cure them." Nelson also asked the Admiralty to send out warmer clothes for the coming winter. He even demanded flannel shirts with longer shirttails, because the men had to lean over so far while out on the yardarms taking in sail during snowstorms.

It was well he took these precautions. By September the storms were again shrieking across the gulf into his fleet. One of his captains, Nelson's third in command, had a nervous breakdown and had to be sent home. Still Nelson waited for the French to come out of Toulon.

For more than eighteen months the long wait went on. For more than a year and a half nearly every man in the fleet stayed aboard his ship, never once setting foot on dry land. Day after day the routine was unchanged. Morning after morning at four o'clock, the starboard watch rolled out of the hammocks, hustling to avoid the smack of a rope end which the mate swung at all stragglers. Until daylight they sanded and scrubbed the decks, cleaned down the ship and polished the bright-work. At daylight the lookouts climbed to the masthead, and at 6:45 came the cry: "All hands, up hammocks!" Every man unhooked his hammock, twisted the blankets and straw mattress (which they called the "donkey's breakfast") into a neat roll. Then each man went to his station at the rail, where the hammocks were stowed in the nettings along the side of the ship. In battle these hammocks would stop a great deal of shot. As the ship was cleaned and readied for another day, the cooks and their helpers prepared the breakfast of "burgoo" (oatmeal), coffee and biscuit. By 8:00 A.M. the mess cooks had distributed breakfast and the men were eating at their tables, slung between the guns on the three decks.

Meanwhile, at the ship's stern, the Admiral was at work in his day cabin. Nelson usually rose with the daylight and said his prayers. His chaplain later wrote that the Admiral was "a thorough clergymen's son. I should think he never went to bed or got up without saying his prayers." Nelson had breakfast, with some of his officers and aides, in his dining cabin at 6:00 A.M. By 7:02 he had taken a quick walk about the deck and was back in his cabin, going through all the paper work required to keep his fleet afloat. There were orders to the captain of each ship, messages and requests to the Admiralty to be carried to England aboard the regular dispatch ships and answers to reports sent in by British agents ashore.

Nelson ordered all the European newspapers his

agents could find, and the *Victory*'s chaplain, Dr. Scott, translated them for him. Dr. Scott had to do most of the reading for Nelson, whose one eye had become so weak that the *Victory*'s doctors would not let him use it for more than short periods. On each side of the Admiral's black leather armchair were pockets, one for unfinished business and the other for finished business. Sometimes Dr. Scott would sneak an unimportant paper from the "unfinished" to the "finished" pocket, because he worried about Nelson's spending too much time on details.

While Nelson listened to the news and the messages and dictated his answers, the ship's company was going through its regular, never-ending practice for battle. Then there was inspection. The officers, wearing white gloves to detect dirt behind any corner, went through the entire ship. But after inspection came one of the high points of the day: grog. A ration of rum mixed with water was issued to every man aboard, while a lively tune was played on the ship's fifes. At noon, as the men slung down their mess tables from the hooks above the guns and sat down for the big meal of the day, Nelson usually emerged from his quarters.

For three hours he would pace the deck. Usually he kept to the quarterdeck, where he could see nearly all of the *Victory*'s rigging and her great spreading sails. In those days there were few man-made things larger than a ship like the

*Victory*, as she rolled across the Mediterranean with all sails set on her towering masts. Sometimes Nelson would tour the entire ship. But wherever he walked, he kept it up until dinnertime, which aboard the *Victory* was 3:00 P.M. Then a drummer beat the tune of "Roast Beef of Old England," and Nelson and his officers gathered around the big table in the Admiral's dining cabin.

On good days a few captains from the other ships in the fleet came over to dine with the Admiral. They dined well because, although they had to keep watch off Toulon, the dispatch boats going back and forth to Gibraltar could bring out fresh foods. So the Admiral's dinner usually included three courses, a dessert and even wines. But Nelson ate little of it. Too much food upset his stomach or made him seasick again. After dinner he would hold conferences with the captains of the fleet, if it seemed necessary, or go over more reports and letters. Then he would return to the deck, to continue his ceaseless pacing. Before nightfall he would walk the deck for five or six hours, covering more than fifteen miles every day. By 7:00 P.M. he was back in his cabin for tea and a bit of supper with his officers. The officers usually had a "nightcap"—a glass of punch and a piece of cake or biscuit—at about 8:00. Nelson often joined them, just before bidding them good-night. He was always in his cot by 9:00.

Always, that is, when things were going well.

But on many of those cold, blustery nights off
Toulon, when the crew had had their second tot
of grog and their supper and the hammocks had
been slung again, the men on the upper gun deck,
swinging in their hammocks and trying to sleep,
could hear the steady footfalls on the planks only
a few inches above their heads. As the green seas
broke over the bows, water dripped through the
planks into their hammocks. Waves washed through
the anchor hawseholes, swishing across the deck
and floating the debris of the livestock pens under
the sailors' hammocks. The *Victory* groaned and
creaked as she worked her way through the heavy
seas. But in the pauses between the groaning and
the swishing and the pounding, the men could
hear it again, sometimes all night long—the steady
thud, thud, thud as Lord Nelson paced his lonely
way back and forth on the deck of the *Victory*.

The *Victory*'s doctors would sometimes wake and
worry too. They knew that Nelson was out there
on the sea-swept deck in near-freezing tempera-
tures, wearing only a light coat which would soon
be soaking wet. And when he returned to his
cabin in the early hours of the morning, he would
kick off his shoes and walk about his cabin in wet
stockings rather than rouse his manservant to take
them off. Officer's stockings in those days were
tightly fitted and rose to the knee, and Nelson

could not remove them with his one hand. But the doctors knew that it did no good to argue with the Admiral about how he was endangering his health; they had tried too many times before, with no success. And so during the first winter of Toulon, Nelson developed a racking cough. It weakened him and made him lose weight, and he could not get rid of it.

The worry and the tension built up as the second winter started. Then, in December of 1804, word arrived that Spain had entered the war, on the side of France. This meant that at least thirty big ships had been added to the French forces overnight. Here was all the more reason to lure the French ships out of Toulon harbor and sink or capture a few of them—if only they could be lured out.

But they refused to leave the harbor. So Nelson tried a new tactic. Leading his fleet over the horizon and down to the island of Sardinia, 150 miles away, he left only 2 frigates behind. If the French, thinking he had gone, made a move to leave Toulon, the frigates were to rush the news to him.

On the afternoon of January 19, 1805, Nelson's fleet was anchored in Agincourt Sound. Launches were ashore filling water casks, and provisions were being unloaded from lighters. Another of the Mediterranean's northwest winter gales was blowing, making the loading difficult and pinning the fleet in the harbor because the wind blew straight into the entrance. At 3:00 P.M. two frigates came racing into the harbor, rolling and yawing as they ran before the gale. At their mastheads, flapping stiffly in the strong wind, were the signal flags: *Enemy at sea.*

There were not more than three hours of daylight left. Nelson knew that he could not sail out of the Sound to the open sea against the gale that was blowing straight into the Sound and the harbor. But there was another exit from the Sound. It was narrow, twisting and strewn with rocks, many of them awash and difficult to see. No ships the size of the *Victory* had ever gone through this passage, and no ships at all had ever done it in bad weather. But Nelson decided to try it.

Through the next hour launches raced out to their ships in reply to the signal that the fleet was getting under way. All gun ports were clamped tight, and the anchor hawseholes were caulked to keep out the smashing seas that the ships would meet outside the Sound. By 4:30 the fleet was weighing anchor, and by 5:30 the *Victory* was leading the way through the passage.

High cliffs shielded the fleet from the worst of the gale, but gusts swooped over the clifftops and threatened to blow the ships off course. Sudden orders were yelled from the bow as a lookout spotted rocks ahead. The call was quickly hallooed down the deck to the helmsman who spun the big wheel, as Nelson paced along the rail near by. Rolling mountains of water surged through the passages and boomed against the sides of the cliffs, sending their spray back over the ships. Wind thundering in the sails drowned out the shouted commands. Sea birds soared down from the cliffs to circle the ships and screech at them.

It was a race against darkness. By six o'clock the *Victory* was burning a signal light, which was answered by the other ships of the fleet strung out astern. Dusk rapidly turned to blackness. The sea hissed and foamed white and the phosphorescence made millions of lights sparkle along the cliffs. But by now the *Victory* was coming out of the passage. Her tall bowsprit plunged under the great seas sweeping into the Sound, and a tumbling cross-chop made her pitch and roll. But she had made it through the treacherous passage, and the entire fleet, each ship following the yellow stern light ahead of her, came out undamaged. By seven o'clock, as a squall screamed across them, the ships rendezvoused in the open ocean, free of the jagged rocks and the white, snarling surf.

The French fleet had finally come out to sea. And Nelson was giving chase.

Nelson had already made his plans. As the last of his fleet came through the narrow passage, he signaled the fast ship *Seahorse*. She was to run down the coast of Sardinia and scout for the enemy, which Nelson expected to be racing down the other side of the island. The rest of Nelson's fleet followed, through the black and squally night. And at dawn Nelson had his ships preparing for the battle he expected that day.

But there was no French fleet to be found. That could only mean that the enemy must be sailing in the opposite direction, down the west coast of the island of Sardinia and east toward Egypt, as Napoleon's ships had done once before. So Nelson planned to run down and intercept them. This time he was sure they would not escape him as they crossed the Mediterranean. He had missed the French once before by not getting between them and Egypt. Now he would be right in their path. But again Nelson made the wrong guess.

What had happened? The French admiral was Pierre Villeneuve, the same Villeneuve who had escaped during the Battle of the Nile. This time Villeneuve had led eleven ships of the line out of Toulon, only to have his fleet scattered by the same gale that had almost pinned Nelson in Agincourt Sound. Villeneuve gathered his fleet together again and was leading them back to Toulon while Nelson was looking for him off the island of Sardinia more than 150 miles away.

So once again Nelson went on a wild chase, all

the way across the Mediterranean to Egypt. Finding no one, he returned to Toulon. He was astonished to discover that the French fleet was still there. Discouraged but still determined, he took up his station again, sailing back and forth off Toulon and waiting for Villeneuve to come out. This time Villeneuve waited only until Nelson dropped over the horizon again. Then, finally, he did come out. And at that point he had a lucky break. Meeting with a trading vessel, he learned where Nelson's fleet was waiting for him. All he had to do was sail down the other side of the chain of Balearic Islands and out of the Mediterranean, without Nelson knowing he had got away.

On April 11, 1805, Nelson still sat in the Mediterranean waiting for Villeneuve to sail into his ambush. But on that day he received news that the wily Villeneuve had gone in the opposite direction. The French admiral was gathering a combined fleet of French and Spanish ships to cross the Atlantic. This was frightening news. If Nelson could not catch up with it in time, the combined French-Spanish fleet could attack and capture Jamaica or the Bahamas or any of the other prized British possessions in the West Indies. Immediately Nelson took off in pursuit, already sensing what a long chase lay ahead.

It was a long chase indeed. As the British ships tried to work their way out of the Mediterranean, the winds blew straight at them, day after day.

Nelson said to one of his captains, "My good fortune seems flown away. I cannot get a fair wind or even a side wind. Dead foul!—dead foul!" So many days did he have to spend fighting these head winds that when he finally did reach the open Atlantic, Villeneuve had a thirty-one-day head start.

Then came a wild and agonizing race through Atlantic storms and frustrating calms. By the time the combined French-Spanish fleet reached the French West Indian island of Martinique, nearly 1,000 crewmen had to be sent ashore for hospitalization. Another 1,000 died before Villeneuve was ready to start back to Europe. In contrast, Nelson lost not a single man during the entire chase.

But many a British crew member was disheartened, and with good reason. Across the Atlantic and from island to island the chase went on, with never a sign of the Combined Fleet. Nelson kept up the game of tag as long as he could and then decided he had better not waste any more time in the West Indies. Villeneuve could have started back across the Atlantic, and this time he might not return to Toulon. He might be following a careful plan of Napoleon's, to join other French and Spanish ships at the English Channel, for the final, all-out assault on the shores of England.

Nelson ordered the course set eastward. And on July 20, 1805, the British fleet dropped anchor at Gibraltar and Nelson went ashore to see if there

were news of the Combined Fleet. It was the
first time he had set foot off the *Victory* in two
years.

There was no news of Villeneuve, so the British
raced on toward the Channel. Then Nelson finally
got a report: the Combined Fleet had returned,
but to the Spanish port of Ferrol, not to the
English Channel. England was still safe from
attack, but only for so long as Villeneuve and his
fleet remained in the Spanish harbor.

Nelson was exhausted. He was weak and sick
from too much tension and too little sleep. He
knew that he had probably saved the British West
Indies, but that was not enough. He was utterly
discouraged by the two years he had spent trying
to catch Villeneuve and make him fight. Nelson
took the *Victory* into Portsmouth for a much
needed overhaul. He was rowed ashore in his
barge. He made his courtesy call on the commander of the port. Then, in a pouring rain, he
climbed into a carriage and set out for home. ·All
night, cramped in the carriage and trying to sleep
on the hard, bouncy seat, he rode through the
dark to Merton. It was 6:00 A.M., and a gray
and cheerless dawn, when he arrived. He felt even
worse than he had when he had written ahead to
announce his coming and to express his frustration
over not catching Villeneuve. "I have brought
home no honor to my country. . . . God send
us a happy meeting. . . ."

# X

## "*VICTORY* MAKE READY FOR SEA . . ."

ORATIO NELSON HAD NOT SEEN HIS home for more than two years. Now at last he could relax and try to forget those wild winters in the Mediterranean while he had waited for the French fleet to come out. Now he could recover from the strain of the long, frustrating chase through the Mediterranean, across the Atlantic and in and out among the islands of the West Indies. Now he could store up his strength for the all-important battle that he knew was to come.

He had owned his estate at Merton for four years. The house was large and comfortable. The grounds were planted with trees of many varieties. A small river flowed through the estate. It was named the Wandle, but Nelson called it "the Nile." There was a walk that led to a summer-house, which he called "the poop," another name for the quarterdeck where he spent so much time pacing up and down while at sea.

At Merton, Nelson could sleep as late as he wanted, while away the lazy hours wandering about the grounds of the estate and forget all the cares of the war at sea. But he was unable to make such a complete change. He still rose in the morning before dawn. And he spent most of his time pacing back and forth at the summerhouse he called "the poop." As he paced, he made his plans for attacking the Combined Fleet.

He did have some time for his loved ones at Merton. These were no longer Lady Nelson and his stepson. They were Lady Emma Hamilton and her daughter Horatia, who was Nelson's goddaughter. Seven years earlier, in Naples, Nelson had stayed with Sir William and Lady Hamilton after the Battle of the Nile. Lady Hamilton had treated his head injury and nursed him back to health. Sir William Hamilton was then Britain's Ambassador to Naples, and both he and his wife became fond of Nelson. They returned to England with him. Nelson found that his many years at sea had drawn him away from his wife. He and Lady Nelson tried to pick up their marriage where it had broken off, but without success.

Nelson moved out of his home and into that of the Hamiltons, who welcomed him. And just before Nelson went off to watch the French fleet off Toulon, Sir William Hamilton died, with Lady Hamilton cradling him in her arms and Nelson holding his hand. Now Lady Hamilton kept house at Merton. She was Nelson's age, and she and Nelson were in love. The Admiral was just as fond of his goddaughter Horatia. Many of his friends and relatives criticized him for leaving his wife, and Nelson himself must have felt twinges of conscience over it. But he never returned to his wife and his rightful home.

On the day after Nelson's return home, he went up to London to make his report to the Admiralty and to discuss the prospects of the coming battle. As soon as he stepped down from his carriage in London, the crowds formed. They cheered him, followed him down the street and reached out to touch him. They also worried about his appearance. He was wasted and thin from his long service in the Mediterranean. His unseeing right eye and the green shade over the other made it difficult for him to see, and he had to walk slowly and with great care, sometimes stumbling over a curb or barely missing a lamppost. Still he walked as erect as any officer in the Royal Navy, and one clerk at the Admiralty noticed that in the courtyard Nelson strode straight across the difficult cobblestones to the doorway instead of following the smoother path. In fact, the clerk said, this was what told him right away that the newcomer must be Nelson himself.

There remained a precious few days of ease at Merton. Nelson's relatives came to see him. Friends he had not seen for years dropped in. A group of merchants called on him to thank him officially for saving the West Indies sugar plantations from being attacked by the combined French and Spanish fleet. There were quiet days by the river Wandle, strolls among the trees and across the meadows of Merton, and games with Horatia, who was four and a half and who could already write a letter and was learning to speak French and Italian.

While Nelson was resting, his enemy was hard at work. Napoleon Bonaparte continued to reinforce what he called his "Army of England," which was massed at Boulogne and other French towns just across the Channel from England. At least 150,000 soldiers, complete with their corps of guides and interpreters, waited for the great invasion. Nearly 2,000 transport vessels sat ready to take them across what Napoleon called the "ruffled strip of salt" to the landing beaches. As many as 25,000 horses were collected for the cavalry charges once the troops were landed. And more Frenchmen were being drafted into the army every day. Napoleon was sure that, once he had forced a landing on England's shores, his army would be large enough to thrust quickly across country to London. Then England—and the rest of Europe—would be his. He had already ordered medals struck to commemorate the event. But to get across the Channel he had to hold off the British navy. He did not have to hold it off for long.

"Let us be masters of the Strait for six hours," he said, "and we will be masters of the world."

This was one reason why he had ordered the Combined Fleet to sail to the West Indies. Napoleon knew how important the sugar plantations of the islands were to England, and he calculated that it would take a week or two before London received the news that Villeneuve had arrived in the West Indies. It would then take at least another week or two before a British fleet could be sent to protect the islands. In the meantime Villeneuve would return to Europe, according to plan, and the Combined Fleet would sail up to the Channel to blast the way for the landing craft, while many of England's ships were still looking for Villeneuve in the West Indies.

This phase of the plan had been foiled by Nelson's chase and quick return; so now the British navy was still watching and waiting off Spain. But if Villeneuve could only sneak out of Ferrol Harbor, slip by the watching fleet and sail up to the Channel, Napoleon might have that short time of protection he needed, before the British fleet could get there. It was autumn, and the tides were right for landings on the beaches. So Napoleon sent an urgent message to Villeneuve as soon as the Admiral had returned from the West Indies: "Make a start. Lose not a moment and come into the Channel, bringing our united squadrons, and England is ours." Meanwhile Napoleon kept before him on his desk a constant reminder of the foe he had to defeat: it was a small statue of Horatio Nelson.

Napoleon Bonaparte was ready, but England also was ready and waiting. Every Englishman knew of the staging camps along the French coast, of the landing craft and the Great Combined Fleet which was preparing to clear a path across the Channel. England's Parliament voted extra taxes to pay for more guns and fortifications. Hundreds of thousands of Englishmen marched back and forth in regular drill, learning how to defend their homeland when the enemy came. Trenches were dug along the beaches. Watches were stationed on the shores, on the lookout for the hordes of French troops that might come over the horizon any day. And in English homes many a naughty boy was told to behave himself, or "Boney" would get him when he came to England. On every high hill between Portsmouth and London, sixty-five miles away, there was a semaphore station. The signal would be passed from one hill to the other when the invasion came.

On September 1 Nelson went to London to

confer with the prime minister. A report had arrived: Admiral Villeneuve had left the harbor at Ferrol. Where was he? The watching British had lost contact. Had Villeneuve taken the Combined Fleet, or part of it, back to the West Indies to attack the islands now that Nelson was no longer there to protect them? Nelson could only guess the answer to the question. His guess was that Villeneuve was still somewhere near England, perhaps in the big harbor at Cádiz. A huge fleet could be assembled there for the final assault.

If this were the correct guess, the British Fleet should lose no time in forming up off Cádiz, ready to fight the Combined Fleet to the death when it came out. If it got by, nothing would stand in its way. Villeneuve could take his great ships of the line rushing up the Channel, to lead the landing boats straight for England's beaches.

The prime minister asked Nelson, "Now, who is to take command?"

Nelson replied, "You cannot have a better man than the present one—Collingwood."

The prime minister shook his head. "No, that won't do. You must take command."

Nelson was prepared for this. He had known all along that his vacation at Merton would be short. The prime minister asked if he could be ready in three days.

Nelson answered: "I am ready now."

In his post chaise he rode back to Merton—to

pack, to make his final plans and to say good-bye to Emma Hamilton and Horatia. On the next day came the news.

It was five o'clock in the morning when a carriage clattered up the drive to the Merton house. Down stepped Captain Henry Blackwood of the frigate *Euryalus*. Nelson was already up and dressed. He walked over to Blackwood and said, "I am sure you bring me news of the French and Spanish fleets, and I think I shall yet have to beat them."

Blackwood said yes, he had news of the Combined Fleet. Nelson had guessed correctly in his talk with the prime minister. The Combined Fleet was in Cádiz, preparing for the invasion.

And already, as Blackwood was bringing the news to Nelson, the signal flags were ruffling in the breeze on one semaphore station after another, all the way from London down to Portsmouth. *Victory make ready for sea . . . Victory make ready for sea . . . Victory make ready . . . Victory make ready . . . Victory . . . Victory . . .*

Friday the thirteenth of September, 1805, was Nelson's last day at Merton. He was up early as usual. It was a warm, sunny day. He strolled among the gardens and trees of Merton. He watched the river Wandle roll softly by. He went alone to "the poop" and paced back and forth as he worked out the last details of the battle plan he would soon be outlining to his captains. He played with Horatia. He talked with Emma, trying not to show the nervousness of the last day. Now that he had to go, he was anxious to be off and get it over with, and he listened for the sound of the carriage even though he knew it was not supposed to come for him until evening.

At dinner he could eat little; Emma could not eat at all. And there was nothing more to say. Then, in the dead silence, came the crunch of gravel in the drive as the carriage rolled to the door. Nelson went to his room to take up the last of his belongings. Before coming downstairs he went into the bedroom at the end of the hall, where Horatia was asleep.

The autumn breeze made the curtains move softly at the window. In the dim light from the hallway he could make out only the slightest rise and fall of the small form under the blankets. For a few minutes, while the busy sounds of loading baggage came up the stairwell, Nelson stood in the dark quiet room, looking down on the slight, sleeping figure. Then he knelt and closed his eyes in prayer. He rose, took a long last look at the small form and walked quietly out of the room.

A few minutes later he had said his last good-byes to Emma. The carriage door closed. A whip cracked. The horses grunted and surged against the traces. The carriage lurched forward and down the drive, spraying gravel onto the lawn. Slumped in the dark corner of the carriage, unseeing, unhearing and utterly alone, Horatio Nelson rode off down the Portsmouth road to the sea.

And through the night the clatter of the racing carriage wakened the townspeople along the Portsmouth Road. Many of them lay awake long after the clatter had died in the distance, wondering who it was racing through the night—and if it meant that England's time of peril had finally come.

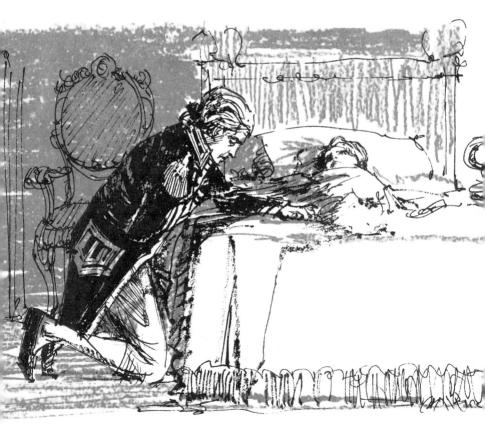

# XII

## TRAFALGAR: POISED FOR THE KILL

HE DARK QUIET OF THE TAVERN IN the town of Guilford was broken by the clatter of hoofs and wheels on the cobblestones as Nelson's carriage rolled to a halt. A startled barmaid bowed to the well-known, one-armed figure and led him to a table for some refreshment while the horses were changed. While he waited, Nelson took out his diary and scribbled with his left hand: "At half-past ten drove from dear, dear Merton, where I left all which I hold dear in this world, to go to serve my king and country. . . ."

Within minutes he was off again. A few hours later, at Liphook, the horses were changed for the last time, while Nelson drank a cup of tea. On south toward Portsmouth he rode, looking out of his carriage window at the slowly lightening dawn. By 6:00 A.M. the carriage was rolling past the familiar buildings of Portsmouth.

The carriage finally came to a stop in front of the George Inn, where a room had been prepared for him so he could catch up on the sleep he had lost on his long ride through the night. But instead of napping he went to the dockyard to pay his respects to the commissioner of the port and to confer with three captains who were waiting for their ships to be made ready. Nelson then returned to the George for another meeting. By noon he was ready to go aboard the *Victory*.

All through Portsmouth the word had spread: Nelson is here! The crowds gathered at the entrance to the George. Hoping to get away without too much fuss, Nelson went out a back door and through an alleyway. But someone spotted him and the crowd rushed toward him. Picking his way slowly past the outstretched hands, Nelson shook those he could reach, apologizing because he did not have two hands to greet more of them. Those who could not reach his hand tried to touch his coat. Then, as he moved through the throng, everyone fell silent. Some took off their caps as he passed. Others dropped to their knees. Others brushed away tears. A few moved their lips silently as they prayed for him.

The Admiral's barge waited at Southsea Beach. The sailors held their oars smartly at attention. As Nelson walked down the steps to the dock, the crowds pushed past the sentries who were trying to hold them back. The barge slid out across the water toward the flagship. And suddenly the silence was broken as the people began to call and cheer. Some of them walked out into the water, still crying his name. Nelson stood in the barge and waved his hat to them. Beside him was Captain Sir Thomas Hardy, the *Victory*'s master. Nelson turned to him and remarked, "I had their huzzas before. I have their hearts now."

Aboard the flagship local officials waited to greet him. There was no breeze, and the *Victory* sat calmly at a single anchor. Unable to set sail at once, Nelson invited the officials to have dinner with him. It was a gay dinner party, with many glasses raised and toasts proposed to success in the coming battle. But after the dinner Nelson beckoned one of the officials aside and confided to him that he had a feeling this battle was to be his last.

With dawn came a light breeze, and by 8:00 A.M. the *Victory* was under way. A boat came out with a letter from Emma, and Nelson quickly scribbled a message: "I cannot even read your letter. . . . The wind is quite fair and fresh. We go too swift for the boat. May Heaven bless you and Horatia. . . . Farewell. . . ." The letter over the side into the boat, which put back for the shore as the *Victory* spread her huge sails to the wind and ran faster down the harbor toward the open sea.

Out in the English Channel the wind turned against her, and the *Victory* tacked back and forth, making slow headway on her course down the coast. As she passed Plymouth, Nelson ordered signal flags flown for the two 74-gun ships that he knew were in there waiting to join him. They were to come out if they could. Nelson did not believe they could, since the wind blew straight

into the harbor at them. But they did manage to make it, and the *Victory* and her escorts set their course—southeast for Cádiz.

It was the evening of September 28 when they arrived off the Spanish coast. The soft September air blew the scent of orange trees out to sea. Studying the harbor with his telescope, Nelson could make out thirty-six enemy warships, "looking

me in the face." He decided to repeat the gamble which he had taken earlier off Toulon. He ordered the watching British fleet fifty miles west, out of sight of the harbor. Here, as at Toulon, he guessed that the enemy would never come out while a British fleet sat waiting in full view. So he led his ships over the horizon, leaving a few fast frigates to stand watch, and took the chance that the Combined Fleet might slip past them. He warned the captain of the frigate force: "Let me know every movement. . . . Watch all points, and all winds and weather, for I shall depend on you."

And as he waited, he prepared for the battle. The next day, September 29, 1805, was his forty-seventh birthday. The sea around the *Victory* crawled with barges and ships' boats as the captains of the fleet came over for a conference. Up the towering side of the flagship they climbed, to the entry port at the middle deck; there they walked aft and up the steps to the upper deck and Nelson's quarters. The Admiral's day cabin ran from one side of the ship to the other, and a long row of sloping stern windows looked out on the sea. It was a clear, warm day, and the sun reflected off the water below to throw wavering reflections on the white cabin ceiling.

Nelson greeted each captain with his left-handed handshake. To one he presented a letter he had brought out from the captain's wife. For another he had good news. Captain Thomas Fremantle's wife had been expecting a baby. Nelson asked him, "Would you have a girl or a boy?" The Captain, who already had two girls and two boys, replied, "A girl." Nelson smiled and answered, "Be satisfied," and handed him a letter. It was from Mrs. Fremantle's sister, announcing that a daughter had been born to the Captain and his wife. Within a few minutes Nelson's cabin was crowded with captains and other officers sitting in the armchairs around the table in the big cabin. As the officers sat and waited for Nelson to speak, they looked about the green-and-gray woodwork of the cabin and at the two huge cannons that stood, one on each side, by the closed portholes. At the head of the table sat Nelson, his slight figure slumped in the deep leather chair, his empty sleeve pinned to his coat, his one good eye staring straight ahead as he prepared to outline his strategy. Inside the cabin, the beams overhead creaked with the motion of the ship. In the distance, far down the deck, a loose cask thumped, and a scurry of feet reminded everyone that this hushed cabin was the heart of a floating community of more than 800 men, and a fleet of more than a dozen ships.

As he thought over his plan of action, Nelson must have let his mind run back to the days when he had paced back and forth in the summerhouse at Merton, planning the tactics for the battle he knew would come. He realized that the

tactics of the Nile and of Copenhagen would not
serve this time. There would be too many ships
in the Combined Fleet for any similar type of
action. Nelson had counted as many as thirty-six
enemy ships in Cádiz. How do you attack and
capture thirty-six ships, even if you have thirty-six
of your own? How do you plan ahead for the
right ships to take on the right ships of the
enemy? How do you make sure that in the confusion of so big a battle your fleet does not get
hopelessly tangled?

More important was the fact that the ships
depended entirely upon the wind. If there were
little or none, the tactics might have to be changed
at the last minute. If there were too much wind,
the guns could not be brought to bear because
of the rolling and the pitching of the warships.
Because of all these difficulties, the British navy
had long ago devised a simple strategy that could
almost always be followed by a fleet in any
weather and under nearly any conditions. The
strategy was to send the entire fleet down the
enemy line, firing as it went. This was what
Nelson had done at Copenhagen, and it had
worked against great odds because of the superior
fire power of Nelson's gunners. His gunners were
perfectly trained and ready this time too. But
Nelson knew that there were too many ships
involved for this kind of broadside-to-broadside
battle. No matter where he stationed the flagship,

it would probably be too far away for many of the ships in the fleet to see his signals through the smoke of battle. But the major reason for not sailing into a broadside-to-broadside battle was that the Combined Fleet had many more guns than the British. There were many more ships in the Combined Fleet, and some of them were bigger than the biggest Nelson had.

How was he to overcome this advantage of the enemy? In his summerhouse at Merton Nelson had figured out a way, and he now explained the plan to his officers. The British fleet would be divided into three divisions. In three separate lines the ships would sail down on the enemy. Instead of swinging alongside the enemy's line, Nelson would try to break through it and split it. When the French and Spanish saw these separate divisions bearing down on them, they would not know which way to turn or how to form a line of defense. No matter which way the Combined Fleet turned, the British could turn the other way and confuse their defense.

So Nelson explained his plan. The British fleet would be divided into separate fleets immediately. They would sail that way from now on so that, no matter when the time for fighting came, they would be ready. And when the battle did come, the commander of each division would be on his own.

This was a revolution in British naval strategy.

Always before the entire battle had been directed by one commander, with the signal flags flown from his flagship. But this time there were too many ships, and Nelson decided to divide the command as well as the fleet. As soon as they went into action, the separate commanders would take over. So the enemy would be faced with separate actions instead of a single one, and would be utterly confused.

As Nelson described his scheme to his officers, they saw immediately that it was just the plan for so large a battle. That night Nelson wrote Emma that the plan went through the conference "like an electric shock." One captain after another said, "It must succeed, if only they will allow us to get at them." The conference ended and was followed by a small birthday celebration. Nelson's steward brought out the wine bottles. The glasses were passed around, and everyone toasted Nelson and victory.

But one day after another went by while the British fleet waited for the Frenchmen and Spaniards to come out of the harbor. While Nelson waited, more and more ships arrived to join his fleet. On October 7 the *Defiance* came into sight, down from Portsmouth. So did the frigate *Amphion*, from Lisbon. Next day came the *Naiad* and the *Royal Sovereign*. By October 14 Nelson could look out from his quarterdeck and count 27 ships of the line, four frigates, a schooner and a cutter.

All waited on the heaving sea off Trafalgar, gathered for the kill.

Then the signal came. It was eight o'clock on the morning of October 20. Aboard one of the British frigates watching off Cádiz the lookouts saw the huge Combined Fleet begin slowly to move out of the harbor—ten . . . sixteen . . . twenty-five . . . thirty-three . . . thirty-eight . . . forty ships covered the horizon with their billowing sails. To the masthead of the frigate went the signal flag: *number 370.* A few miles away, barely in sight, the next frigate in the line passed the message on: *number 370.* And through the British fleet over the horizon the message ran like wildfire: *number 370.* No one in Nelson's fleet had to look in the signal code book to know what 370 meant. It meant: *The enemy's ships are coming out of port.*

Horatio Nelson sat at his desk, scrawling with his left hand a note to Emma Hamilton: "The signal has been made that the enemy's Combined Fleet are coming out of port. We have very little wind, so that I have no hopes of seeing them before tomorrow. . . . I hope in God that I shall live to finish my letter after the battle. May Heaven bless you. . . ."

That was at noon on October 19. All that afternoon, all that night, all the next day he watched for some sign of the Combined Fleet. But

Admiral Villeneuve had run into trouble. His fleet was so large that he was having a great deal of difficulty leading it out of Cádiz Harbor in a blustery wind. As his ships moved their way out to sea and tried to form a line of battle, the British frigates watched their every move and signaled to Nelson over the horizon. On the afternoon of the twentieth, Nelson told his officers, "The twenty-first of October will be our day." Back to the frigates went the order to watch the Combined Fleet every minute and not let it get away. "If the enemy are standing to the southward, or towards the Strait [of Gibraltar], burn two lights together, every hour, in order to make the greater blaze. If the enemy are standing to the westward three guns, quick, every hour." And even before dark, at 5:00 P.M., the frigate captains signaled that the enemy was standing southward. Nelson ordered the British fleet to turn in a parallel direction.

He would still stay out of sight, so Villeneuve would not be frightened back into Cádiz. With the winds and weather so changeable, the Combined Fleet might slip past him, as it had at Toulon. And if Villeneuve and his mighty fleet escaped Nelson this time, they could race for the Channel and pave the way for the invasion of England. But Nelson accepted the risk, in return for making sure Villeneuve would come out far enough to fight.

It was a warm, sticky, gusty night. The *Victory* plowed southward through the dark. From the quarterdeck Nelson could see all around him the riding lights of his fleet, rolling with the heaving sea. Every hour, over the horizon to the east, the sky would light with the eerie blue flash of the signal lights. His frigates were still keeping the enemy in sight. An answering rumble of guns from Nelson's fleet told the frigates that their signal had been seen and that the British were still watching and waiting. And belowdecks, throughout the *Victory*, Nelson could hear the preparations for battle.

Bulkheads were being taken down, so that each deck was one clear space with no interrupting walls. Tables, chairs and all other movable objects were carried down to the hold or made ready to tow astern in boats during the battle. This was because a cannonball could split a table or chair into huge flying splinters that could drive through a man like so many spears. Everywhere there was the rumble of the big guns rolling back and forth as they were tested against their restraining gear. Nelson went to his sleeping cabin, now partitioned only by a hanging curtain. He undressed and climbed into his cot, which hung on ropes so as to swing with the roll of the ship. Exhausted by the anxious wait, he dropped off to sleep at once. And as his sleeping body swung from side to side in the hanging cot, the porthole of his cabin lit up every hour with the blue Bengal fires, signaling that the enemy was still running south.

Before dawn, as the cot rolled more heavily from side to side, Nelson woke. He jumped down and started to wash. His steward heard him and brought him a hot drink. Dressing quickly, he went up the steps to his quarterdeck.

There was only the faintest light in the eastern sky. The gusty winds of the night had died out. Only a light breeze dappled the sea. But a heavy swell was running in from the west—huge, slowly rolling hills of water sweeping through the fleet and making the *Victory* rock and creak and groan. Now another blue Bengal fire lit the sky, not so brightly this time as the blackness gave way to a pale gray. Nelson studied the situation with satisfaction. Finally he had the enemy in a trap. Villeneuve had sailed too far through the night. In this light breeze he could not run back to Cádiz. This time he would have to fight.

The sky slowly brightened into blue and the sun made a golden band across the horizon. Nelson, and every other man in the fleet, watched the sea to the east, straining to make out whether they had come close enough to sight the enemy fleet themselves. And as the morning mist moved away, there it was—a great long line of ships, their masts looking like a floating forest as they sat almost motionless on the windless sea. Just beyond them, too near for comfort, rose the jagged cliffs of Cape Trafalgar on the southwest coast of Spain.

Nelson called for his signal lieutenant and told him to hoist the signal to swing into battle order. Because of the lack of wind, he had the fleet form two lines instead of three. As his signal was answered through the fleet, the British ships turned toward the enemy line of battle. Then, at 6:25 A.M., Nelson called to his signal officer again to hoist number 13. Up to the masthead it went, and on every ship in the fleet the signal officer reported it to the captain: Flagship signals, *Prepare for battle*. As the order ran through the fleet, Nelson studied the enemy through his telescope. He could see that the Combined Fleet was much bigger and more powerful than his.

Now the breeze flickered and died completely. At this rate, Nelson estimated that it would take five hours or more before he would reach the Combined Fleet. But there was no telling when the wind might come back. This was why Nelson had given the order to prepare for battle. It was a long process. All the furniture that had not been taken below was piled into the ships' boats, which were lowered and strung out astern. Men swarmed through the rigging, carrying chains to fasten the heavy yardarms, so they would not come crashing down if their rope slings were shot away. Water casks and fire buckets were placed about the deck, to be ready in case of fire. Nets were slung along the sides to repel boarders. Below, along the great lines of guns, the cannonballs were stacked; and "powder monkeys," boys in felt slippers that would not strike a spark, rushed back and forth carrying flannel bags filled with gunpowder. Blankets were hung around the powder magazines. They would be soaked with water to help protect the powder from any fires near by.

The gun ports were opened and closed to make sure they were ready. The heavy lines that held the guns in place and checked their recoil were inspected. Below, on the deck at the waterline, ships' carpenters collected the wooden plugs that would be hammered into any holes shot in the ship's side. New tackle was strung near the tiller, so the ship could be steered if the wheel were shot away or smashed. And on the lowest deck the ship's surgeon and his helpers prepared their instruments for the bloody work they would have to do when the wounded were brought below. Alongside the surgeon's operating table stood large wooden tubs. These would measure the grisly price of heroism—in the numbers of arms and legs the surgeon would have to amputate.

The breeze did not pick up. Nelson paced his quarterdeck, stopping to watch the Combined Fleet through his glass as it tried to come about and head north. Apparently Villeneuve had de- cided to make a run for the harbor after all. But

Nelson knew that the enemy commander had made his decision too late. With not enough wind, the French and Spanish ships could make no headway. They slatted about and formed a ragged, crescent-shaped line, headed north but going nowhere.

As Nelson stood watching them, Dr. William Beatty, the *Victory*'s surgeon, approached Captain Hardy, the *Victory*'s master. Dr. Beatty was worried about Nelson's safety. The Admiral was wearing the uniform coat he had worn ever since coming aboard the *Victory*. The coat had embroidered decorations on its left breast, and Beatty thought they made too good a target. There were sure to be sharpshooters in the enemy's tops. Beatty asked Hardy if the Admiral shouldn't be asked to change his coat for one that would attract less attention. Hardy answered that he did not think the Admiral would like being told to change his coat, even for a reason like this. But he promised that he would mention it if he got a chance.

They were still three or four hours away from the enemy, drifting slowly down toward the ragged line, with every sail spread to the wisps of air that wafted across the gently heaving sea. Nelson decided that it was time for a last inspection of the *Victory*'s battle stations. His steps crunched in the sand that had been spread on the decks to keep them from getting slippery when covered with blood. On the gun decks he studied the short carronades, the guns that were called "smashers." They were being loaded with round shot and musket balls, which would spray like gigantic buckshot across the enemy decks. Other guns would fire chain shot, which would whip around anything it hit. Others would fire fagot shot, pieces of iron that would slice enemy sails and cut away rigging. But the *Victory*'s most powerful weapon was her massed series of "32-pounders," which could throw a great 32-pound cannonball with enough force to drive it through a hull a mile and a half away. Around these guns stood the gunners, stripped to the waist and wearing handkerchiefs around their heads. When the firing started, they would slip the handkerchiefs over their ears so they would not be deafened by the roar. As Nelson approached, they paused in their work. "My noble lads," Nelson said, "this will be a glorious day for England." The men gave him a cheer and went back to their work, as he climbed down the steps to the next deck.

By the time he had returned to his quarterdeck it was 10:00 A.M. The sea was still calm, with only a fitful breeze. Off against Cape Trafalgar the Combined Fleet looked as if it were sitting still, waiting for the attack. Nelson studied the enemy, looked around at his fleet again, and went below to his cabin. It would not be long now.

Lieutenant John Pasco, the *Victory*'s signal officer, had expected to be the ship's executive officer by now. His rank entitled him to this office, but somehow the promotion had been overlooked. Now Lieutenant Pasco came to Nelson's cabin to deliver a message and to ask if he could be given his proper promotion while someone else took over the signaling assignment. He walked into Nelson's day cabin, and stopped in his tracks.

Admiral Nelson was on his knees, his back turned to Pasco and his head lifted as he offered a prayer for victory in the coming battle. Lieutenant Pasco forgot all about his complaint. He waited until Nelson rose to his feet, then delivered his message and withdrew.

A few minutes later Nelson appeared on the quarterdeck again. And now, at his signal, Captain Hardy turned to the ship's first lieutenant. "Mr. Quilliam," he said, "send the hands to quarters."

The First Lieutenant called to the drummer who was standing ready. "Drummer—beat to quarters!"

Like an explosion the booming sound of the drum went through the ship. The drummer marched up and down the deck, pounding out the signal. And in the farthest corners of the *Victory* the call echoed and reëchoed: "All hands to quarters! All hands to quarters! *All hands to quarters!*"

The ship seemed to burst. Hundreds of men rushed across decks and up and down stairways to their stations—at the guns, along the rail, down to the orlop deck where the surgeon was preparing for the wounded. Others hurried to stow the last of the ship's gear that would not be needed in battle. Others filled buckets and doused the decks, hammock nettings and sails to avoid fire. Finally a tense silence fell on the *Victory*, as she rolled slowly toward the great enemy fleet.

The breeze picked up slightly and the *Victory's* sails filled. Still she moved at only walking speed. All around her the other ships spread their sails as the breeze moved them forward with the flagship. Now the two British lines of battle moved toward the Combined Fleet. The clouds upon clouds of canvas made a majestic sight, and one of the British captains called his officers on deck just to see the spectacle. They had seen nothing like it before and probably would never see anything like it again. Aboard the *Victory* the men on deck noticed that the smooth water around the ship was cut by the fins of sharks, circling and waiting.

Nelson swept the enemy fleet with his telescope again as the ships drew nearer, studying the crescent-shaped line of battle and trying to determine the best spot to hit. Near the center of the line was the *Santissima Trinidad*, her lofty sides painted in stripes of red and white. She carried 130 guns and was much larger than the *Victory*; in fact, she was the largest ship in the world.

Nelson guessed that this must be the enemy flagship. The *Victory* headed straight for her.

Nelson turned to one of his officers and said, "I'll now amuse the fleet." He walked across the quarterdeck to where Lieutenant Pasco, the signal officer, was standing. "Mr. Pasco," he said, "I wish to say to the fleet, 'England confides that every man will do his duty.'"

As the signal officer, Lieutenant Pasco of course knew by heart what each signal flag meant. Not only did some flags stand for letters in the alphabet, but others stood for numbers, and the British fleet carried a code book in which each number represented a particular word. Lieutenant Pasco knew that in the code they were using there was a number for each word in this message except the words "duty" and "confides." He replied, "If your Lordship will permit me to substitute 'expects' for 'confides' the signal will soon be completed, because the word 'expects' is in the vocabulary and 'confides' must be spelt." Nelson nodded. "Make it directly."

Lieutenant Pasco gave the order. The flags went fluttering up the halliards, and through the fleet the signal officers of the other ships repeated it: "253: ENGLAND, 269: EXPECTS, 863: THAT, 261: EVERY, 471: MAN, 958: WILL, 220: DO, 370: HIS, 4: D, 21: U, 19: T, 24: Y."

Aboard the *Royal Sovereign*, leading the other British line off to the south, Admiral Cuthbert

Collingwood watched the signal flags rippling in the light breeze. He muttered, "I wish Nelson would leave off making signals. We all know what we are about." But as the message was translated by the signal officers of the fleet and passed among the crews, a chorus of cheers could be heard floating back across the water. If Nelson heard them, he paid no attention. Now he said, "Make the signal for Close Action. And keep it up."

On the *Victory*'s deck a band struck up a battle march, "Britons Strike Home." When the march was completed there was a hush. And across the water the British could hear the faint sound of a French band playing "The Marseillaise." The enemy was battle-ready too.

# X I

# TRAFALGAR:
# THE FINAL, TRAGIC TRIUMPH

T HE ROYAL SOVEREIGN, LEADING THE second battle line toward the Combined Fleet, had a new copper bottom, and was sailing faster than any other ship in the British fleet. The *Victory* might have sailed faster if she had gone into dry dock for repairs while Nelson was ashore; but she had been ordered to stay at anchor, ready for sailing immediately if necessary. So now Nelson stood aboard the *Victory*, watching the *Royal Sovereign* draw near the enemy line. As the Admiral watched, Captain Hardy took the opportunity to mention the coat and the decorations. Wouldn't they attract enemy sharpshooters? And wouldn't it be a good idea to change? Without turning, Nelson said he guessed so, but it was too late now. This was no time "to be shifting a coat." As he watched, the *Royal Sovereign* came within range of the enemy and opened fire.

The growling broadsides could be heard across the water, and the smoke rose from the sides of the ships as the *Royal Sovereign* closed with the Combined Fleet. She hit the line at about its middle. In a shower of cannonballs and clouds of smoke, she cut the line in two. Behind her came the British ship *Belleisle*. It was exactly noon on October 21, 1805, and the Battle of Trafalgar was on.

Nelson was still watching the first British line plow into the enemy fleet, when the distant sound of a splash caught his ear. He looked across the bow of the *Victory* and saw the widening circles. The enemy had opened up on him.

As he watched the Combined Fleet, a row of red spots flashed down the sides of the enemy ships. Smoke rose from the gun ports. Just ahead of the *Victory* the water splashed as the shots fell short. Only a few minutes later the enemy gun ports flamed and smoked again. There was a deadly whir as the cannonballs flew overhead. Holes suddenly appeared in the *Victory*'s sails. The enemy had "bracketed" her—fired both ahead and astern of her. That meant that the gunners of the Combined Fleet would now be able to figure the *Victory*'s range. There were a few tense moments before the next enemy broadside. Then it came, right on target.

Sails flapped as halliards were cut. Huge splinters, nicked off the masts and spars, shrieked across the deck, spearing every man who stood in the way. The air was filled with bits of rope and cloth as the hammock nettings were scattered by the shot. And the first of the many wounded were carried below to the surgeon on the orlop deck. The first man hit was Midshipman John Poilard, the signalman who had hoisted the "England Expects" flags at the order of Lieutenant Pasco. Pollard was slashed in the arm by a flying splinter, but he refused to go below. He tied a bandage around the wound and picked up a rifle to use when the *Victory* came closer to the enemy.

Now the *Victory*'s gunners checked their cartridges, their rammers and sponges and their cannonballs. As they pulled their handkerchiefs up around their ears, they could hear the gunners' mates shout the order: *Make ready!*

The flintlocks were cocked, and the gun captains looked through the gun ports for the target. But there was no target yet because the *Victory* was still heading straight for the enemy line and had not swung around into firing position. That would come as soon as the *Victory* hit the enemy line, which would be within minutes.

Nelson and Captain Hardy stood together on the *Victory*'s quarterdeck. "Starboard a little," Hardy said softly, and the order was repeated to the helmsman. The *Victory* swung to the right and aimed for a hole in the line astern of the French ship *Bucentaure*. Now, as the *Victory* came closer to the enemy, the air shrieked with cannonballs and chain shot. Nelson's secretary, John Scott, walked up to make a report to Hardy, and suddenly fell to the deck, cut almost in two by a shot. The marines quickly picked up the body and tossed it overboard before the blood made the deck dangerously slippery. Whipple, the captain's secretary, took Scott's place, only to be killed a few minutes later. Another enemy broadside sent whirring lengths of chain into a company of marines mustered near the quarterdeck; eight fell dead. Nelson turned to the captain of the marines and called: "Disperse your men round the ship." He thus saved the marines from further slaughter, but at a greater risk to his own life. Later the marines could have helped protect him from the sharpshooters in the enemy tops.

The Combined Fleet kept up the fire, barrage after barrage, as fast as their gun crews could load and fire. A salvo smashed through the hammocks in the nettings at the rail; it sent bits of hammock flying, splintered the ship's launch and chipped pieces of wood from a mast. One of the pieces cut off a buckle on Hardy's shoe. Nelson and Hardy looked at each other, and Nelson said, "This is too warm work to last long."

Another shot smashed the *Victory*'s wheel, and the ship veered out of control for a moment, until helmsmen below could rig the steering tackles that had been prepared for such an emergency. The enemy was also aiming high, in hopes of hitting the *Victory*'s masts. One of the high barrages now struck the *Victory*'s mizzen topmast. It groaned, snapped and toppled over. Crewmen went at the tangle of rigging with axes to clear the mess away. But still the *Victory* did not return the enemy's fire.

At the rows of guns on the decks below, the gun captains watched tensely as the *Victory* rode nearer and nearer to the enemy line. In the pauses between enemy broadsides they could hear the shouts of the French and Spanish gunners and the rattle of blocks as the guns rolled back against their restraining gear. And now at last the *Victory* began her slow turn.

She was aiming to pass across the stern of the French ship *Bucentaure*. They were about fifty yards away from her. The distance shortened to forty, then thirty yards. The gunners watched the high stern slowly approach. They would pass within a few yards of her. Now it was twenty yards, and the bow of the *Victory* was crossing the *Bucentaure*'s stern. The *Victory*'s guns were double-shotted—filled with twice the normal load. Near the *Victory*'s bow were the carronades, loaded with round shot and 500 musket balls each.

Slowly the tall French stern came into range, the sunlight glinting off her stern windows. Then at last, aboard the *Victory*, came the order: *Fire!*

The *Victory* rocked as her broadside went off. Hundreds of pounds of iron, chain and musket balls screamed through the stern windows of the *Bucentaure* and swept the length of the French ship. French guns were knocked over. Gunners were mowed down. As the *Victory*'s gunners raced to reload and fire again, they could hear the wild screams of the enemy wounded. Through their gun ports they could see the French lying in piles all over the deck. Three hundred men aboard the *Bucentaure* were killed in that one broadside from the *Victory*. And as the *Victory* moved past the *Bucentaure*'s stern, great black clouds of dust and flying wreckage drifted down on her from the shattered enemy ship.

Nelson's plan of action was working. Already he had cut the enemy line in two places, and had turned the battle into a churning struggle instead of one long line of ships firing broadsides at each other. Now every ship could fight for itself, and the Combined Fleet had already lost its advantage of having more and bigger ships.

But the *Victory* was fighting for her life. Just beyond the *Bucentaure* was the big French ship *Redoutable*, and the *Victory* headed for her. In the close quarters of the battle there was no way for the two ships to swing off and fire at each other; they simply crashed together and bounced off. But as they did, the *Victory*'s yards caught on those

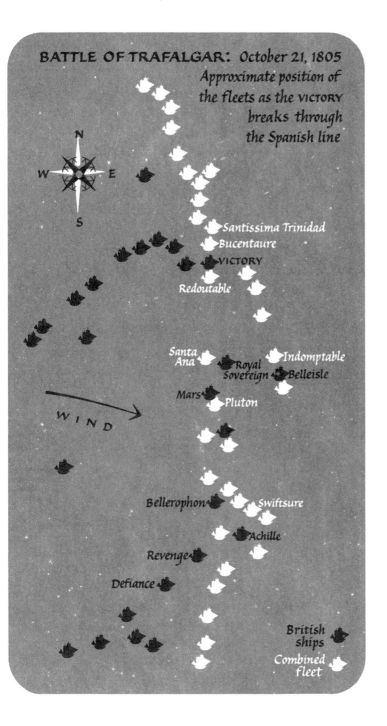

**BATTLE OF TRAFALGAR:** October 21, 1805
Approximate position of
the fleets as the VICTORY
breaks through
the Spanish line

N
W E
S

Santissima Trinidad
Bucentaure
VICTORY
Redoutable

Santa
Ana
Royal
Sovereign
Mars
Pluton

Indomptable
Belleisle

WIND

Bellerophon
Swiftsure
Achille
Revenge
Defiance

British
ships
Combined
fleet

of the *Redoutable* and they were locked together. The ships were so close that the *Victory*'s gunners were firing into the *Redoutable*'s gun ports, and were receiving fire the same way. Here again, as at the Nile and Copenhagen, Nelson's gun-crew training proved its worth. Almost always the *Redoutable* was hit by two broadsides for every one she fired. But on the *Victory*'s quarterdeck it was different. The *Redoutable* had riflemen hidden behind canvas screens in her masts, and they were covering the *Victory*'s deck with a withering fire.

Still Nelson and Hardy continued to pace back and forth. Nelson would not go below; his place was on his quarterdeck, and he would not desert his post. So the two officers strode from the shattered wheel to the hatchway. (It was seven paces from the wheel to the hatch.) Then they turned and walked the seven paces back, side by side, the tall figure of Captain Hardy beside the short frail one of Admiral Nelson. They were just about to turn at the hatchway when Hardy realized that he was alone.

He turned and saw Nelson on his knees, leaning on his left arm. Then the arm gave way and Nelson fell. Hardy and the sergeant major of the marines reached Nelson at the same time. As Hardy kneeled beside him, Nelson said, "Hardy, I believe they have done it at last."

The sergeant major and two seamen gently lifted Nelson to carry him below. Nelson pulled a handkerchief from his pocket and draped it over his face and the decorations on his coat; he did not want his men to know, at the height of the battle, that their admiral had been shot. But on the middle deck he removed the handkerchief long enough to look at the steering cable rigged to the tiller and ordered that it be tightened. He replaced the handkerchief as the seamen struggled down the last blood-slicked steps to the orlop deck.

The cockpit, as this section of the orlop deck was called, echoed with the cries and groans of the wounded. At least forty men lay waiting their turn. A few lanterns dimly lit the scene. Huge shadows danced against the bulkheads and on the deck, which was painted red to camouflage the blood that flowed during battle. One of Nelson's bearers slipped and almost fell, but caught himself in time. A surgeon's assistant took one look at the uniform where the handkerchief had slipped away, and shouted: "Mr. Beatty! Lord Nelson is here! The admiral is wounded!"

As Surgeon Beatty came to meet them, the handkerchief fell and he saw the pale face of Nelson. At his orders Nelson laid on a mattress and his clothes were quickly taken off. A sheet was pulled over him, and Beatty felt his pulse. It was still strong. Then the doctor examined the wound and tried to probe for the bullet, while Nelson gritted his teeth and held his breath. Beatty could not find the bullet; it had gone too deep. He looked at Nelson's back, but could find no break in the skin. The bullet had lodged somewhere near the backbone.

"Tell me your sensations, my lord," the doctor asked.

"I feel a gush of blood every minute. . . . I have no feeling in the lower part of my body . . . breathing is very difficult and gives me very severe pain about the part of my spine I am sure the ball has struck. . . ."

As he listened to these symptoms, Beatty's heart sank. He knew what had happened before he heard the Admiral say, "I felt it break my back."

While Beatty tried to soothe him, Nelson asked him to go and attend to the other wounded. "You can do nothing for me. I have but a short time to live. . . ." Dr. Beatty assured Nelson that his assistants could care for the others. But Nelson ordered him to return to his operating table.

Nelson closed his eyes and listened to the sounds around him. From the decks above came the stamping of the gun crews, the lumbering sound of the guns as they rolled back and forth, and the thunder as they fired. In the dim cockpit there were the groans of the wounded, the cries of the young midshipmen unable to fight back tears, and the sudden piercing shriek of a man whose arm had to be cut off without any pain-killer except a gulp of rum. When Nelson opened his eyes, he could hardly see. He asked for Captain Hardy.

For a moment the guns seemed to go quiet. Then there was a distant sound of cheering. Nelson asked, "What is that?"

Pasco, the signal officer, had been wounded too, and lay near Nelson. He raised himself on his elbow and said, "Another enemy ship has struck, my lord."

Nelson smiled with satisfaction. But then a spasm of pain shot through him. He called for a drink, and was given a sip of water. Beside him knelt the *Victory*'s chaplain, Dr. Alexander Scott, and the purser, William Burke. "The enemy are decisively defeated," said Burke, "and I hope your lordship will live to be yourself the bearer of the joyful tidings to our country."

Nelson replied without opening his eyes. "It is nonsense, Mr. Burke, to suppose I can live. My sufferings are great, but they will soon be over."

Then he asked again: "Will no one bring Hardy to me? Has he been killed then?"

He was answered by the clear young voice of a midshipman still in his teens. The midshipman had been taught the proper way to address an admiral, and he did not forget his training, even in a time of stress like this. Taking a full breath, he repeated the message exactly: "Circumstances respecting the fleet require Captain Hardy's presence on deck. But he will avail himself of the first favorable moment to visit his lordship."

A hint of a smile appeared on Nelson's lips. He tried to see the messenger but could not make him out. He asked who brought the message. Burke whispered to him, "It is Mr. Bulkeley, my lord."

Nelson's mind went back to that day in London when his old comrade from the San Juan campaign had brought his two sons to see him. Even now he could see young Richard Bulkeley standing in his parlor, gazing with awe at the shining naval sword. Young Bulkeley had enlisted in the navy and had come to sea aboard the *Victory*. And here he was delivering his message in the heat of the battle.

Nelson said quietly, "It is his voice." To the young midshipman he said, "Remember me to your father." Richard Bulkeley tried to answer, but his voice choked with emotion and he stumbled off to return to his battle station.

Nelson closed his eyes again, clenching his teeth as the pain shot through him. Burke lifted him gently so he could lean against the bulkhead in a half-sitting position. For a while this made him feel a little better. Dr. Beatty came to look at him again, but could do nothing to relieve his pain.

Finally the tall figure of Captain Hardy came clumping down the steps. Bent forward to keep from hitting his head on the low beams, Hardy strode over to where Nelson lay. He took Nelson's hand.

"Well, Hardy," said Nelson, "how goes the battle? How goes the day with us?"

"Very well, my lord. We have got twelve or fourteen of the enemy's ships in our possession."

"I hope none of *our* ships have struck, Hardy?"

"No, my Lord, there is no fear of that."

As they talked, Dr. Beatty came up. Hardy turned to him and asked in a low whisper if there were any hope. Beatty opened his mouth to reply, but Nelson spoke first.

"No. It is impossible. My back is shot through. Beatty will tell you."

Hardy looked at Beatty, who nodded silently. Hardy took Nelson's hand for a moment. Then, without a word, he turned and climbed back up the steps, to carry on the direction of the battle.

Dr. Beatty returned to his work. A few minutes later he was back to ask how Nelson felt. Nelson told him, "All power of motion and feeling below my heart are gone."

Beatty was silent for a moment, and then said softly, "My lord, unhappily for our country, nothing further can be done for you." Nelson replied in a whisper, "I know." Dr. Beatty walked a few steps away and wiped his eyes. Behind him, Nelson murmured, "God be praised, I have done my duty."

There was silence, then a sudden crashing, rocking broadside from the *Victory*. The ship swayed and shifted Nelson. He gave a soft moan. "Oh *Victory! Victory!* How you distract my poor brain!"

The heavy shoes of Captain Hardy came down the steps again. The Captain walked slowly over to the mattress, reached down and took Nelson's limp hand in his.

Nelson opened his eyes but could not see. Hardy

announced that he had come to congratulate his lordship "on a brilliant victory, which is complete." The enemy had been thoroughly beaten, and at least fourteen ships had been taken.

Nelson smiled and whispered, "That is well. But I bargained for twenty."

Then, remembering the long swells that meant an approaching storm, and the nearness of the rocky Trafalgar coast, Nelson said, "Anchor, Hardy. Anchor."

Hardy nodded. Nelson was quiet for a minute before he said, "I feel that in a few moments I shall be no more. . . ." There was a long pause, and he said, "You know what to do. And take care of poor Lady Hamilton."

He tried to take a deep breath, but could not. His lung, punctured by the bullet, was filling. He was drowning in his own blood.

Hardy stood looking down at the frail figure. Here was the man who had crushed Napoleon's navy at the Nile, the man who had smashed the enemy coalition at Copenhagen. And now he had saved England's very shores by destroying the most powerful fleet that had ever set out to attack his homeland. His historic mission was accomplished, and he lay dying.

Hardy knelt, bent over and lightly kissed Nelson's forehead.

Nelson's good eye flickered but did not open. "Who is that?" he asked.

"It is Hardy."

Nelson whispered, so softly he could hardly be heard: "God bless you, Hardy."

Captain Hardy rose slowly, walked a few feet away and held onto a beam to steady himself. Then he straightened up and climbed swiftly up the steps to the deck.

And as Dr. Beatty tried in vain to feel the Admiral's pulse, Nelson moved his lips slowly: "Thank God, I have done my duty."

Fifteen minutes later Nelson's steward came to Beatty, who was tending another of the wounded, and asked him to return to Nelson's mattress. Beatty felt Nelson's wrist, put a hand on his forehead and then told Chaplain Scott that he could stop massaging Nelson's chest. There was no need for it any longer. Vice Admiral Viscount Horatio Nelson was dead.

# XIII

## SILENT TRIBUTE

N THE DECK OF THE VICTORY MID-shipman John Pollard was firing his rifle at the enemy aboard the *Redoutable*. The two ships were still locked together, the battle still went on. It was the same Midshipman Pollard who had been wounded after hoisting Nelson's signal and who had bandaged himself so as to stay in the battle. A movement up on the *Redoutable*'s mast caught Pollard's eye. About twenty feet up, behind a strip of canvas stretched around the mast top, a French rifleman stuck his head up and fired at the *Victory*'s deck.

Pollard ducked behind a bulwark, leveled his rifle and waited for the man to show himself again. As the Frenchman stood up and aimed his musket, Pollard fired. The Frenchman dropped. Pollard reloaded. Another Frenchman tried to scurry down the rigging. Pollard fired again and the man fell to the deck. Nelson's death had been avenged.

For only a short while longer the shooting went on. Little by little the roar of battle died down, as one enemy ship after another was put out of action. Then the French *Achille*, set afire by British broadsides, blew up in a thundering explosion and a cloud of debris. The Battle of Trafalgar was over. Horatio Nelson had won his greatest victory, at the cost of his life.

He had saved England. The Battle of Trafalgar smashed Napoleon's greatest threat. With twenty-seven British ships Nelson had attacked thirty-three enemy ships, many of them larger than his, and had beaten them all. Not a single British ship surrendered. And of the few French and Spanish ships that managed to escape capture, none could ever go into battle again. Once and for all Napoleon had to give up his dream of assaulting England. No longer did Englishmen need to post watches along the beaches and drill militia in the towns. When his great Combined Fleet was beaten by Nelson, Napoleon turned his attention in the other direction. He marched inland, against Russia, where he met defeat. And finally he fought the British for the last time in the famous Battle of Waterloo. But it was Trafalgar, ten years before Waterloo, that made England safe.

Yet Englishmen everywhere found it difficult to celebrate the great victory; their grief over the loss of Nelson was too great. Everywhere in England, as soon as the news reached home, women put on black and men wore mourning bands around their arms. Even as far away as Naples, people were overcome by Nelson's death. The poet Samuel Taylor Coleridge wrote that, as he walked the streets of Naples, Italians who recognized him as an Englishman came up to him, took his hand in theirs and burst into tears.

In the British fleet the feeling was even stronger. One sailor wrote home about the battle and reported his surprise at seeing men who had fought so bravely now crying like girls. The new commander of the fleet, Admiral Collingwood, ordered that Nelson's body be taken home aboard the frigate *Euryalus*. When news of the order reached the *Victory*, there was a near mutiny. The men of the *Victory* had served directly under Nelson; they had fought beside him; many of them had been in the dark cockpit with him when he died. They wanted the honor of taking his body home to England. Collingwood listened to their request and changed his order. Nelson would go home as he had come out, aboard the *Victory*.

But first the *Victory*, like the other ships of the fleet, had to put into port for repairs. Her mizzen top was gone. Much of her rigging was shot away. She had countless holes in her sides, and despite new patches she leaked a foot of water an hour. With her men working constantly on the pumps, she rode out the storm Nelson had predicted and made her way to Gibraltar, towed part of the way by one of the less damaged ships. At Gibraltar she was repaired enough for the voyage home. Then, through more autumn storms, she sailed for England, with the body of Admiral Nelson in his cabin.

On December 4, 1805, at six in the morning, the *Victory* came in sight of Portsmouth once more. It was eighty days since she had weighed anchor and sailed from Portsmouth for the Battle of Trafalgar. Now she was home again, her flag at half-mast. The day was cold and gray. Squalls roughed up the sea and made her roll and pitch. She had to anchor for shelter and more repairs before she could continue on up the coast. It was

December 23, two days before Christmas, when she finally reached Greenwich, on the outskirts of London. There the officials from the Admiralty came out to receive Nelson's body.

Aboard the *Victory* was the cold hush of death. The visitors' steps echoed in the stillness. The coffin was brought aboard. It had been made from the mainmast of the *Orient*, the great French ship that had blown up in the Battle of the Nile; one of Nelson's officers had had the coffin made then, and Nelson had saved it for this time. The small body, dressed in full admiral's regalia, was placed in the coffin. The Union Jack was draped over it. As the coffin was lowered into the royal yacht, Nelson's flag was lowered from the *Victory* for the last time, and raised to half-mast aboard the yacht. Bells tolled. Minute guns boomed. The yacht carried Nelson's body across the river to Greenwich's Painted Hall, where it would lie in state.

So many people tried to crowd into the Painted Hall, where he lay in state, that many were hurt in the crush, and troops had to be called out to control the crowds. Then, on January 8, 1806, the king's state barge was taken down to Greenwich and given over to a picked crew from the *Victory*. Nelson's body was put aboard the barge, and Nelson's men rowed their admiral on his last voyage, up the river to London.

There, in a funeral procession of 160 carriages, England's hero rode through the streets of London to St. Paul's, where he was to be buried. Fifes and muffled drums played the "Dead March." The wheels of the hearse crunched through gravel that had been sprayed along the route. From the thousands upon thousands of Englishmen along the streets came no sound save a murmur and the whispering rustle of hats taken off as Nelson passed by. At St. Paul's, Nelson's men waited with the *Victory*'s flag, which was to be lowered into the grave with him.

But then, at the last moment, they could not do it. As the coffin was laid in the grave and the drums rolled and the final minute guns were fired, Nelson's men grabbed his flag and tore it into shreds. Each man took a bit of the flag for himself and stuffed it into his shirt—as a personal memento of the man everyone would always remember as England's greatest hero.

AUTHOR'S NOTE

IF YOU HAD BEEN A SCHOOLBOY IN ENGLAND about a hundred years ago, one of the first books on your required reading list would have been *The Life of Nelson* by Robert Southey, England's poet laureate from 1813 to 1843. This is a small, beautifully written book, and it is still available today (Dolphin—paperback: New York, Doubleday & Company, Inc.; Everyman's Library—hardcover: New York, E. P. Dutton & Co., Inc.). If you want to read more about Nelson, this is the book I recommend above all.

But there are many other good books, including:

*Victory, the Life of Lord Nelson* by Oliver Warner (Boston, Little, Brown & Co.: 1958).

*Nelson the Sailor* by Captain Russell Grenfell (New York, The Macmillan Company: 1950). This one is particularly good if you are interested in the tactics Nelson used in his different battles.

*Nelson* by Carola Oman (New York, Doubleday & Company, Inc.: 1946). This is probably the most complete of all the popular biographies.

*The Life of Nelson* by Captain A. T. Mahan (Boston, Little, Brown & Co.: 1897 & 1900). Though more complex, this book contains facts and points of view that many of the other biographies don't have.

If you are more interested in the battles than in Nelson's

life, there are some excellent books on two of Nelson's battles. One is *The Battle of the Nile* by Oliver Warner (New York, The Macmillan Company: 1960). Mr. Warner has also written a good book on the Battle of Trafalgar, titled simply *Trafalgar* (London, B. T. Batsford: 1959). By far the best book, however, on the Battle of Trafalgar is *Decision at Trafalgar* by Dudley Pope (Philadelphia & New York, J. B. Lippincott Company: 1960).

If you would like to read a little more about Nelson's times, try *Nelson's Captains* by Ludovic H. C. Kennedy (New York, W. W. Norton & Company, Inc.: 1951) and *Sea Life in Nelson's Time* by John Masefield, another of England's poet laureates (New York, The Macmillan Company: 1925).

But better than all the books in the world is a visit you must promise yourself even if you have to wait years before you can make it. In Portsmouth, England, only a couple of hours by train from London, sits the great old ship herself, the *Victory*. She has been preserved just as she was at the time of Trafalgar, and you can go aboard her and be guided through the ship by a young British seaman who knows the *Victory* thoroughly and loves her as only a British seaman can. As you pace the quarterdeck, stand in the wide captain's cabin or climb down to the red-floored orlop deck, you can all but hear the ghost of the great man himself—walking the deck above you, speaking crisply, "Mr. Quilliam, send the hands to quarters" or, in the soft sad whisper of approaching death, "Thank God, I have done my duty."

A.B.C.W.

# INDEX

# Index

# Index

# Index